UNNECESSARY ROUGHNESS

GROWING UP AFRAID, OVERCOMING BULLIES
AND ACHIEVING SUCCESS

WENDELL P. HAYWOOD

Kim
To a great neighbor
and friend. Enjoy!
Wendell P, Haywood

CONTENTS

ACKNOWLEDGMENTS

I want to thank my mother for her genuine way of loving me the best way she could. Our relationship is fantastic today and as a son, I couldn't ask for anything better between parent and child. The climate of my early life as well as that of my mother's was marred by uncontrollable circumstances. This situation affected the normal parent-child relationship that should possess tenderness, bonding, and expressions of love.

Joy and happiness did occur but unfortunately, not until well into adulthood. It was a time when life spooled out darkness about us and thus, between us. I didn't understand or know what love was or what it was meant to be as a kid.

Today, I love my mother with genuine gratitude, understanding, and respect for the life she lived and sacrificed for her children. We talk and laugh as if we were brother and sister separated by oceans but tuned in to a kindred spirit over the airways.

To my sisters, who growing up were madly independent, fighters and guardians of family—sometimes escorted back home by police and many times, they were the ultimate warrior princesses. Rebels, perhaps. Despite some light to middle weight unsanctioned fights well beyond what a brother and sister are expected to have (we fought and yelled like alley cats), I'm forever grateful to be able to call them sisters. I love them dearly, for helping me to understand and accept the value of family. They're still crazy and bossy in their own grown up way but they've succeeded in life. I love them despite the punches and kicks that defined our rivalry growing up.

I'm thankful to the quiet inspiration from my brother, who set the example by making it out of the projects alive. He played his clarinet and saxophone in the D.C. Youth Orchestra and made it to a performance in Switzerland. It was through him that I knew it was possible to jump over the wasteland and live the undiscovered truth of a world outside of 15th Place.

Many thanks to my bro, my cousin Daryl. He gave me a place to go (his room) and a best friend to hang with. We ran for fun, occasionally were chased by the law, sang in the choir (he was good, and I was along for the ride although my baritone voice could vibrate the choir chair in front of me), shared good friends, and commiserated in our pains and hopes.

We even graduated to the point of finishing each other's thoughts. I lived vicariously through Daryl for a long time, looking up to him (just one year older) as the mature person, even though we were both just kids. Daryl was able to live and thrive in a place worse than my street. He always had a job, girlfriends and a fiancée in the making. I don't recall anyone messing with this big strong dude. I was invincible, too, whenever we hung out together. He provided me cover until I finally came into my own at the end of high school. Bros always!

A special thanks to Sarah Quah with her savvy writing experience and insights. She kept me true to my inner self while guiding me through the fine art of writing. A special thanks to my editor, Charlene da Silva, for translating my words into the world of book publishing. Her expertise and cover design made a difference, and carried through the finish line.

PROLOGUE

"There was never yet an uninteresting life. Such a thing is impossibility. Inside of the dullest exterior three is a drama, a comedy, and a tragedy."

— Mark Twain, "The Refuge of the Derelicts"
(1905)

"I wish they would just lock them all up and throw away the key," an acquaintance once said in reaction to the unrelenting increase in numbers of dead bodies stacking up at the hands of brazen murderers. The thought was even more telling,

"I wish they were all dead."

This was during the early in the 2000s. The District of Columbia was well on its way to becoming the country's "murder capital". That low title was attained without much competition. My thoughts lurched back to a time when I often thought, "I hate this life." Nonetheless, I was quick to defend my birthplace.

I convulsed at the harsh hearing of what others thought of my hometown. Only those who lived in D.C. proper the ten square miles which defines the district bordered by Maryland and Virginia—had the right to pound a gavel-pronouncing sentencing for an entire city. Short of that jurisprudence—it was my birthright and my decree to bring the city to an end. It was an inheritance, though unwanted, that was being dismissed without permission.

Second to this dark, hidden feeling of hating my life and "wanting them all dead" was a thought that resembled a low-lying, ominous fog that endured and obstructed the view of future and hope. Why should they continue to live if existence was based on how much pain and fear could be inflicted? My real-life experience said I was the prey, though I did not fall victim to a brutal act of murder or savagery. Something more insidious and uncontrollable was perpetuated without an end in sight. It's implausible to accept that at five or six years of age that I could have seen this veil covering my life.

I couldn't consciously express it but knew there was something pressing down hard and unrelenting, beating that kid that was me into submission, into becoming that which was loathed even by those who inflicted the daily hurt and shame. Could it perhaps have been my destiny to accept that I, too, was a "project boy," akin to public supported or inner-city housing existence of the 60s and 70s? Perhaps the time had come for me to accept that there was no escaping that inheritance. A nerdish and bookish appearance was not a pass or warrant. Beat the nerdy kid too— what did it matter? What reward might that kid earn to elevate him from Dante's *Inferno* to above the clouds of despair?

Robbing, mugging and bullying that kid was needless and uncalled for. He was a neighbor—the kid who sat with his assaulters in the same classes yet was forced by brute intent to surrender his possessions and dignity. What was the threat or objection I posed in the lives of my abusers?

Thus, the title—*Unnecessary Roughness*—became the perfect analogy for life during an impressionable age. I am embarrassed to admit that I didn't realize the sports relevance of the book's title. It seems everyone else immediately knew grabbing a player by his face mask, head butting, clotheslining or kicking an opponent is considered unsportsmanlike conduct and unnecessary roughness. Such actions usual result in penalties and can involve monetary fines. One explanation suggested such conduct is a sign of lack of discipline. It all makes perfect sense–*Unnecessary Roughness: Growing Up Afraid, Overcoming Bullies and Achieving Success.*

My memoir about these infernos below, takes place on the blacker side of Washington, D.C.—the southeast section of the District of Columbia on the perch of what was called home on 15th Place. This was the inferno from elementary to junior high school. This book represents an eclectic group of seared memories which collectively helps to, at least, explain how I became the Wendell P. that I am today.

The place may be different for you, but it really could be your story as well. The scenery of your abyss could be the harsh reality of being fifteen years old and three months pregnant. Maybe you're the recovered addict who used drugs to evade everything but never truly escape anything or suffered the barrenness of a loveless life since your first cry out of the womb as an infant. Regardless, the feeling of hate, sense of embarrassment, and resulting deep-seated ache within the soul is a shared story.

You, like me, were zipped into an environment that was tight, itchy, and sticky like a wool body suit on a blistering thick, steamy hot summer day in D.C. Everyone knows the fit is wrong, the timing uncontrollable, and the look of being out of place. It's obvious that you don't belong, and you're not wanted although the justification is always illusive.

Can one survive the heat and sickness of the projects? This "project boy" did make it out alive and succeeded despite the roughness or maybe because of the roughness. Those experiences helped to shape who I am today. I carry sharp pieces of that place and time, like broken glass in my pocket. They served to unexpectedly prick or stab at me as a reminder of a life akin to face masking, clotheslining and unnecessary jabs. Those mental and emotional shots are also hinting of the possibilities of what can be accomplished when adversity and odds are weighed against success.

These, too, speak about specific chances as you also did more than merely survive. You might not have sung inspirational songs about. perseverance or wrote lyrics announcing the act of hanging on by fingertips and a prayer.

In fact, you are not under-privileged or unable to contribute positively to family and society. You and I became comrades in a common cause of resilience and personal triumph. You can become someone too if you haven't made it there yet.

INTRODUCTION

I started this story first and foremost as a means of recording my thoughts about growing up in a public housing project in my very own inner city of millions—black and proud. Actually, I wasn't at all certain about claiming my blackness and less confident of what to be proud of. After several starts, I had an epiphany and rebirth of my premise. I realized my story represented more of a self-prescribed therapy—the ensuing pages seeking to help understand and maybe find words to explain the "whys" of what makes me what I am.

Certainly, the idea begs the question of "who exactly am I?" Might there be a deeply concealed conviction primed to startle family and friends? Perhaps my mental tomb once opened to the light of day becomes the seed for personal inspiration and motivation. Conversely, opening the crypt to pages could be demotivating, or, even worse, a written course of despised self-awareness, fear, and self-deprecation. It all seemed so uncertain to me at the time.

My search for self-expression continued. I later attempted a stream of rewrites, not knowing if colorful and unique revelations would appear. I searched for even deeper purpose with renewed enthusiasm and with a bit of economic loftiness and social notoriety in mind. I might become a newly minted shining author and subsequently a novelist poised for introduction to the literary world. Surely Oprah or "The View" anxiously waited for the next bright star that had to be me. It is my destiny, or so I convinced myself.

I read somewhere that one of the prerequisites of fame has to do with luck and timing. Unfortunately, neither quite synched with my idea of arriving "just in time." Oprah ended her network television reign and became ostensibly the OWN (Oprah Winfrey Network). "The View" kept changing hosts so I couldn't comfortably determine whom best to carry my mantel of success to the television world. My hopes were crushed even before finishing this very paragraph:

"Whoopi, what should I do?"

I recognized my ego, immaturity, and faulty thinking. But I have another confession. I was hesitant and, frankly, terrified that there might be a modicum of success from my story. The pressure of writing an encore, which invariably meant finding more words and creating another unreasonable and unnecessary stressor. Again, my egomania took hold. Penning thought to paper was relegated to a dusty back place in my mind.

Starting anew and returning to my original awakening, I hunkered down with a resolve to simply translate into words the very vivid and searing images of a particular time in my life, a difficult stretch to recall and describe – elementary school through junior high school. This shaped and continues to represent the "who" in "who am I?" After some introspection and honest self-chiding, I decided it best to find satisfaction with simply using this book as a more humbled expression of my attempt to heal "thy self".

Might this be considered a memoir or transcript? Perhaps it's more like an epithet to what was. Or is it a memory exhausted and dried out like fine leather inexplicably found in the scorching and humid tenants of an inner-city row house or a third-floor apartment without central air or an occasional breeze? Yeah, I lived that too. I'm sort of reaching with a coat hanger, twisting and angling through a narrow channel of a dirty cast on my broken life to scratch at a persistent and unwanted irritation. Relief is so near and expected but always seemingly out of reach.

I asked myself, "what would anyone find interest in reading about the life of a skinny black kid from the projects of Washington, D.C.?" The book, movie, and television show has already been made ten times over. I'm no JJ, Cliff, Dewayne, or a kid who made it out and up to own fourteen fast food or dry-cleaning franchises. I'm sure I don't have the hoop-spa of the "three C's" (convincing, compelling and commanding) or even a bright proposal that can be made to defend why you ought to find intellectual intrigue in my story. By the way, the "three C's" was my idea.

I can only state as a matter of fact: this is my story. It's real, and I need to get it out of me.

To do so might just inoculate you and me from the jungle warfare, which stalks thoughts and causes one to question whether doubts will be permanently etched in one's mind. There is an ever-present sense that I was ill-prepared to enter this wilderness which injured and produced awkwardness in my life for a very long time. It was unnecessary roughness for any child. Yet in the long run, it somehow helped a boy lost in a harsh place to become someone more than he was, to find himself and become a man.

I think you know what I'm referring to. The trauma and severity are not unique to me. Nevertheless, many of us have inexplicably been driven to the same familiar edge and wondered how to survive this day or this life. It's happened to you or someone dear to your heart.

"Oh my God!" are usually the first words uttered, followed by a litany of hushed or whispered talk carrying the same predictable and bewildering tone.

"Her life is ruined," they muttered following the news about Samantha's pregnancy at age sixteen—the shame her parents will encounter.

James was sent out of state for drug rehab and whispers trail with certainty that "He will never be the same."

There's a late-night call from an unsympathetic and official-sounding voice announcing your spouse has been arrested for another DUI. In-laws are finally able to verbalize what they felt all along, *"how could my daughter be so stupid to marry him in the first place?"*

My story, though different in space and time, has nonetheless been as life altering as those scenarios just mentioned. National statistics support predictions of my likely failure to contribute to society due to my impoverished beginnings.

> *"Nearly half of all children with a single mother — 47.6 percent — live in poverty. Indeed, the children of single mother's experience poverty at a rate that is more than four times higher than kids in married-couple families."*

"Black children are more likely to live in poverty than children of any other race. The poverty rate among black children is 38.2 percent, more than twice as high as the rate among whites. The poverty rate for Hispanic children is 32.3 percent."

"Twenty-four states and the District of Columbia have poverty rates higher than the national average of 15 percent, with the majority of the nation's poor situated in the south."

— FRONTLINE, NOVEMBER 20TH, 2012

What chance did I have, living in the projects, suffering inexplicable harm, or unnecessary roughness, of being raised with four other siblings by a single mother?

Yet I somehow became an exception and proved the statistics wrong. Though, there was never any celebration or victory dance. There was never any reparation or acknowledgement of my survival and service. Now over five decades later, reliving it helps to move me beyond my demilitarized zone. I was always positioned between likely conflict and actual conflict. This was my war neighborhood and home for far too long both mentally and physically.

My experiences, the outside view of my inner world, are presented in segments or snap shots because these are the fragments which surface so repeatedly in my thoughts. They must have meaning since I could not seem to discard their very crisp negatives and repeated images. Other frames have remained deep in the vault or have disintegrated, leaving me with blank spots and reels of cellulose film coiled tightly ready for showing but lacking content or memory.

So, what memories I do have are strong and forever fused in my thoughts as much as I despise the realities of those reminders?

"I would wrestle, fight, kick and even bite an ear off to keep this Love & Hate (not really much love) imbedded in my DNA."

I understand a condition that occurs called "phantom limb sensation" which may be triggered by several things, including emotional stress. It goes something like this:

When a person loses an arm, he may still feel the presence and sensation in that arm, such as an itch or ache. There is a real physiological thing at work in your mind that directs you to scratch the itch even though your eyes can see there is only the stub of an arm.

Now, I'm all grown up and living the American dream. I have five wonderful boys, four grandchildren, and two ex-wives. At one point, I also had two houses and two mortgages (a divorce thing), lived in six different states, and had a fantastic but challenging career. Yet, what I still have within me is this little "project boy". Although decades ago, the boy became a grown man. So maybe you can understand why I need to tell my very personal story. It hurts to share it—but there is inspiration and motivation here as well. As you journey with me, there's a chance you, too, will be able to relate to the course of your upset life. Perhaps I will be a reminder of how you rose above and climbed the barricade the world said couldn't be overcome.

Thank you for joining me and congratulations on reaching beyond your "unnecessary roughness." You're an over-comer too.

— WENDELL P.

1

SNAP SHOT

I MENTIONED IN THE INTRODUCTION HOW SEARED MEMORIES WERE like snapshots into my life. I would like to keep that analogy going. I see this as the perfect time to tell you a little of where I am now before telling where I've been. I hope to bring you a little context. It's my way of looking through the lens of one frame, which sets the cellulose film securely in the sprockets of the projector before rolling backwards into my life. This is my left-handed, right-brain-version of coming through the back door only after entering a side window on the far corner side of my life. Honestly, I believe my mind would not allow me to address those fears and experiences directly.

My snap shot shows how I've unwittingly strolled into this point of my mid-life, like a child without a nap running unhinged through a maze of the world's largest jungle gym. I'm actively swinging around and climbing over things but to anyone glancing at the chaos of my play—my whole life builds upon itself, thereby, giving a semblance of purpose and direction. I think that's acceptable and earned at this point. Hey! I made it through more than half my life without really knowing where I was going.

This former East Coast boy of a big inner city now lives surrounded by thousands upon thousands of acres of corn and soy bean fields—all located in the heartland of this country. It's a twin city with a population of 125,000 people combined with a county population of over 170,000 people. I work within the financial services arm of a historic and major insurance company.

My nearly thirty-seven years with the same company started with me as a trainee just out of graduate school in Ohio. I only completed half a semester as a grad student exhausted with the thought of more education. I've lived in several states making my way across the country from the east coast to Colorado and back to the mid-west.

Humbly, I am a classic example of starting from the bottom and working my way up to the top of the very department where I started as a life insurance underwriting trainee. Somewhere close to mid-career, I might have had ability and stamina to climb a few more rungs in the professional later but decided living close to four out of five sons after a divorce was paramount for their emotional and mental health. In all honesty, the sense of stability and centering might have been more for me than for them. However, I did it for the boys. Yeah, that's my story. Mr. Jones, my junior high school history teacher, or Mrs. Norwood, my high school math teacher, could not have foreseen this timid Wendell guy carrying responsible for hundreds of people with annual budgets in the tens of millions.

The snap shot of my current position and accomplishments stops there. I tried to continue with descriptions and explanations of responsibilities, politics, current mentors and the complexities of working in a large corporation, but my mental frames forced a different path. Instead of budgets and business travels, money as a kid was top of my mind. I suppose like most kids managing a budget was uncomplicated and straightforward, "you got money, you spent the money you got". However, during my childhood, there was barely any money to receive or handle. I'm not sure when I first learned about the word, allowance. What little money I did have (in the form of lunch money or spare change), most times, was confiscated (nice way of saying robbed) before making it through the doors of elementary or junior high school.

Back then, I didn't realize the world could be any different than a nearly all-black population from an educationally, economically, and culturally deprived standpoint.

Yet I left with a consciousness and recognition that I would be forever different according to standards held by others. I felt scrutinized and came to accept being closely eyed was a result of being who I was—black and later, African-American. It was reasonable considering I lived in a place which didn't seem to examine others so critically.

There were those who assumed Neighborhood Watch status simply because of my mere presence. Sometimes it was the result of a wrong turn down an unfamiliar street where apparently every vehicle is registered in a nationwide database for that street. I was not known, therefore, heads turned, eyes focused and conversations ceased until this boy was out of the wrong neighborhood. I used to think as a young teenager why wasn't I mistaken as a friend of a friend, a co-worker, gym teacher or church member.

Although these situations still occur today, they tend to be more positive than negative. Most people will at least wave or smile with direct eye contact, acknowledging your presence. Granted there is an invisible line in which suspicion replaces friendliness.

A similar experience occurs today when I stray down an unknown street in a black neighborhood. The difference is that the stares received tend to be a moment of wondering if I'm a friend or relative. I have experienced a difference with my own people once the housing prices moved into a high and exclusive margin. It seemed to return to the level of suspicion or the "I've got mine and you're not going to steal it either" look. Even socio-economics can be a contentious rod within a group of people.

I too was one of those who stared at the uncommon and unknown person making his way through my exclusive public housing subdivision. Somehow an invisible logic, call it "project sense," accurately announced or warned you when someone didn't belong. Other not-so-neighborly folk saw potential opportunity.

Maybe it wasn't so much a mystical or innate connection with the universe as opposed to recognizing certain practicalities about car ownership in my world. For example, no one in the neighborhood drove anything that wasn't at least ten to fifteen years old, by my estimation. That was a new car to me. Cars were scratched up, dented, sometimes with huge depressions in hoods or trunks, and windows replaced by plastic and duct tape. The norm included the obvious body panels and parts barely held together despite significant rusting from every seam.

Keep in mind that many of those dents and bangs were the result of friends sitting and leaning on the cars; kids running around and invariably into them (at least that's what I did) and the nonchalant parking lot ding afforded any well used car. What was the "dingee" to do anyway? Today one might consider exchanging insurance information with the "dinger." During my time in the projects, few had exchangeable information due to the lack of money that afforded those conveniences. You opened your door and hit someone's car. Then, you went on into the corner store.

A hanging tailpipe or ruined catalytic converter might have served as another sign of being black. When any vehicle appeared to be a new model (no dents, scratches, and doors all the same color) came down the street, it became an automatic eye-catching event. If that person were white, then he was either working for the government or out of his lost damn mind.

That's when I learned of and saw a certain sound of fear that wasn't from me. I certainly had my fears and reasons for it, however, this isn't the sound I'm referring to. It's the protective sound of metal chambers and gears activated resulting in the well-known echo of all doors being locked in an impenetrable position. Have you ever heard the metallic thud of security? It's difficult for the lost white person to appear casual and uninterested when there's this loud and heavy swooshing sound of metal securing the driver from the outside world of blackness all about. I can't count the number of times that's occurred in my life. Oh, so now I carry a menacing and threatening persona because of the color of my skin? I could have really used this in junior high school.

It was not unusual to be an outsider even in my own neighborhood in the projects. It was as if I were another race or ethnicity who wandered naively and haphazardly into danger. One would think my black skin would summarily issue me some kind of "pass" card in Anacostia, the southeast part of town or parts of the northwest where we black clearly commanded little but dominated, nevertheless. Blacks got what we wanted. I'm just not sure what it was. Nevertheless, we could get it if we really wanted it. I learned later that equal opportunity and financial equality were at the top of the list that usually found blacks at the bottom whether because of gentrification or the hope that one day it will be my turn.

For me that wasn't the case. My nappy afro and common skin color didn't make a difference. I could easily be seen as a threat to something within the walls of my neighborhood. Perhaps it was a nice stereo or TV set. I'm certain it wasn't my nerdy look, which carried fear and loathing. It was more likely that my scrawny bookish look attracted a menace and gave something to do for so many who just seemed to be there, hanging out as if waiting for a tire to be changed on the car they didn't have. I learned where not to stray even as a kid in my own southeast corner of the District of Columbia.

My snap shot is that of a man with a successful career but carries a history that is always present. I'm reminded in part by society and the socio-economics that define upper and lower classes. More insidious are the reminders that played out in the experiences that shaped me. Some were real and stinging while others, due to their absence, represented a deeper hurt and uncertainty.

I thought someone's name could even be a "cause & affect" directing respect or pain. Did my name prop up my survival chances? Sometimes a name conveys strength, distinction or respect in the projects. What chances did I have if it all comes down to a name?

2

IT'S ALL IN THE NAME

HAVING BRIEFLY DESCRIBED THE SNAP SHOT OF MY PRESENT position in life, I'm stuck with trying to understand and explain where I came from and what I use to be or what I am. I remember the somewhat quaint soliloquy that goes something like:

> "[Insert your name] was here but now he's gone, he's left his name to carry on."

I've concluded you can't leave all the experiences that encompass and comprise the backbone of a person's given name unless you have a starting point and horizon to reach for. A name is more than just the letters it consists of. It is more of the tapestry woven throughout one's early years, which truly reflects who was here and what he or she left as a reminder and legacy. In my case, I'm still here so there is hope for me yet to deposit something besides a friendly smile, a pleasant social demeanor, and a well-known weakness for certain candy bars.

By the way, I still like the uniqueness of my name and how I share it with people of historic and impactful standing. I asked my mom one day how she'd come up with my first name—Wendell. "I don't know," was her response. I queried her nonetheless, "Was I named after a relative, a well know actor, blues artist, an Underground Railroad conductor, or someone famous?" Each creative, hopeful comparison was met with either a resounding "no", "I don't know", or "I don't recall." I had to be somebody and not just made up at the moment.

My name has recognition even today. How many times have you been likened to or caused others to reflect on, at least in name, former famous negro athletes, poets, orators and champions like Oliver Wendell Holmes, Wendell Barry, American Poet, Wendell Smith, Arna Wendell Bontemps, and Wendell the Great (I may have made that one up). I don't recall the name of another Wendell in school until I reached college. That exclusivity also made it easy for certain others to know me as the guy who should be punched in school hallways after the bell rang, signalling time to change classes. I looked like a Wendell—I was bookish, eager to learn and, yes, nerdy.

I've yet to see a guy with my name who looked tough and ready to curse a parent or threaten a teacher. I expected that from a Cortez, Leroy, Darvon, Ronnel, Marvis, Curtis, Butch, Bobbi, Damon and other evil, demonic sounding names. These are normal sounding names today, but they were my tormentors as a kid. I didn't know anyone named Francis, Doug, Jerry, Pauly or Tom until around my early-to-mid-twenties. One would have to work exceptionally hard to have earned an intimidating demeanor with a first name such as Tom. I suspect a Tom would have to murder one Doug and mug or maim at least two Francis's in order to gain his props and earn my lunch money. Even I have standards.

I think we may have had a few terrifying names in school that sounded strangely like the southern arm of a mafia family. Vito Ritzuto had to start training somewhere so why not in the D.C. public school system? One would eagerly forfeit lunch money, paper, pens, and notebooks. (don't know why they wanted them since I never saw any of them write) to someone named Donnie or "Big Finger". He was a real tormentor. His thumb was curved like the shape of a banana that reminded me of the handle of a machete. I'm guessing the "Big Finger" was the result of a genetic or birth defect. He was not the usual heavy dark-skinned heft of a guy with facial hair patched into a beard more becoming of a resident of a maximum-security prison. Donnie was light skinned who spoke with a lisp and walked like one of the cool dudes from the B-movie *Cotton Goes to Harlem*. He could beat the crap out of you and often did. I knew of Donnie not only because of the oversized thumb that you dared not stare at, but also because he was one of the alleged drug pushers in elementary and later junior high school.

I remember movies with bullies acting out. The word itself sounds too weak and diffident compared to what I came to expect as a kid. The movies would show a bully forcing another kid into writing a homework assignment. Yes, I was once one of those kids ordered by Donnie to write a paper due for some class. The boy could barely read any more than write so what teacher would not have known immediately that this was not his work?

How does one negotiate a way out of this situation? I vaguely remember pausing after the casual demand or was it more of a command. What the hell was I going to do? If I didn't write it, a beating would ensue. If I suggested it was not right for me to do that, then a beating would follow. If I said anything other than ok, then—you guessed it—a beating would naturally occur. I now see how logical and practical I had become at such an early age. Perhaps, I just didn't know at the time whether I would survive to parley this learning into something more constructive. I'm glad that situation occurred only once. Admittedly, I didn't understand why it didn't happen more. I supposed seizing money was more direct and rewarding.

I do clearly remember listening to Donnie, Cortez, and a few others in class being called on to read aloud. He stumbled over enunciating basic words such as "that", "achieve", "physical", or "physically". The only thing missing was the dramatic musicality arriving in waves of deep and resonating base drums pounding out the beginnings of a crescendo that never arrives. It's as if a few percussionists in the New York Philharmonic Orchestra took a restroom break in the middle of the maestro's wild swing of his baton. Something was missing.

You would think one would be just about half way through pronouncing a word such as "physically" just right. It would invariably end up sounding like the phonetic equivalent of "phi-sic-call-lee". Everyone in class knew not to look at or make eye contact with these guys. Surely, a person gazing in disbelief would incur the warning of a beating to be followed by the actual beating at the end of school. I saw this happen a few times, so I easily avoided that misjudgment.

Teachers would not utter words of correction or even encouragement. They also knew the reality that would await them at the end of a school day. I'm convinced Donnie and his boys were illiterate in its purest meaning, yet they made it through grade school (out of sheer terror of what would happen if they were not graduated). Most teachers knew not to act as if they were teaching our in-house thugs. These dudes knew what car a teacher drove. An insurance company would only repair or replace a ride so many times. Tires would be slashed, or windows busted. I've known a time or two when a teacher was jumped and badly beaten. I know of only one occasion where after such a beating did the teacher return to the school. I can only imagine the post-traumatic stress some may have carried for decades as a consequence of molding young minds.

I should note there was some semblance of respect or chivalry in that guys would beat up male but not female teachers. They left that up to the girls. Some girls were scary as demons and appeared to no longer demonstrate female traits. Male hormones, once suppressed, overpowered any feminine nature. These girls were as badass as the guys. Some were even worse.

It wouldn't be unusual to find a girl weaving and throwing a jab or left hook with the same effectiveness as Marvin Hagler or Sugar Ray Leonard. I'm not sure who would beat up teacher's aids but luckily for them we never had any nor did we have any volunteer parents. Are you kidding? For the most part there were no volunteer parents even at home. School was a convenient dumping ground for the unwanted while welfare checks were collected, and babies were delivered so that more welfare checks could be had. This was a true "circle of life". In many ways the city was saying "Hakuna Matata" from the movie *The Lion King*. It meant no worries for the rest of our days. No one cared so why worry?

My mom, however, cared. And she stayed after us about school and housework. A belt whipping met the backside of whoever was the under-achiever. There was great persuasive power in the specter and force of the belt, the switch, or whatever was handy. I had to go outside a few times to select my own beating branch. I took a lot of care and focus to ensure I got the weakest switch and to find something without thorns or stickers. I never came back with a branch from a rose bush. I was nerdy but not stupid.

Thank goodness none of the "Donnies" made it past junior high school. Surely it became impossible to pass them up the educational ladder. I suspect a simpler explanation. I wonder if drugs proved more profitable than lunch money. Funny, those names aren't so intimidating (although not completely removed from my subconscious even today) as they were when I was six to ten years old. I heard as an adult that Ḍonnie was murdered. I had no feelings and didn't care or know what became of all the other Donnies from the streets around 15th Place southeast D.C.

3

LIVING IN THE BIG LETTER E

"It is often easier to become outraged by injustice half a world away than by oppression and discrimination half a block from home."

— CARL. T ROWAN

ON ONE OF MANY TRIPS BACK TO VISIT FAMILY IN WASHINGTON, D.C., I followed my personal triumphant ritual of driving through what was my nemesis. I'm not sure one can refer to an entity or an entire housing project area as an archenemy. Nevertheless, that inanimate place was alive with a soul. There was something organic with a dynamic presence only seen through the microscope of that life which survived.

I was always drawn to return to what could be thought of as the scene of the crime. Visits would shine a harsh light rearward, retracing something within me against my better judgment. The blaring intensity of that reflection blocked out the memory of anything else and forced me to relive, if only briefly, some parts of what was and of that which never quite faded away. The environment of my canvas had already been painted, and I was thrown into it on 15th Place. I don't recall much else except a few flashes of parents fighting and a ride in another country with my dad. Wikipedia describes public housing:

> "Originally, public housing in the U.S. consisted primarily of one or more concentrated blocks of low-rise and/or high-rise apartment buildings . . . and housing projects have also been seen to greatly increase concentrated poverty in a community."

Whoever wrote that statement apparently had visited the public housing where we dwelled. First, allow me to describe this place called home. It was located on a straight long street. I'm not sure how people referred to the buildings. Today, they would be replaced with and described as neatly manicured and well-situated row houses or town homes. I guess you could call them condominiums too.

The description that now stands in place of the courts and the dozens upon dozens of manufactured cutouts came from a poorly designed city plan. I likened it more to a master baker who was missing several fingers, had a gangrenous eye, and only five baking instruments. They consisted of three hammers, one screwdriver and one "thing-of-a-ma-jig". Now, imagine what came out of the oven.

EACH COURT WAS SHAPED LIKE THE LETTER E WITHOUT THE middle stem. The photo at the start of the chapter doesn't do justice. This inner-city landscape was a crisscross of cracked and crumbling sidewalks, connecting units to one another in a court. Their neatly planted borders were really pathways or ruts coursed through plain and lifeless dirt. That's right—dirt or the stuff Mother Nature never intended to be used except for prison exercise yards or abandoned roads found under bridge abutments. Weeds grew without challenge.

I don't think pure Kentucky Blue Grass ever imagined there would be a chance to thrive. Weeds claimed their parcels much like an animal marking its territory. Nothing else grew—yet one could always find jagged rocks struggling free of this encrusted landscape. They seemed to be competing with shards of glass from Colt 45 and other beer bottles or the neighborhood favorite, Boon's Farm wine.

Occasionally, a monstrosity of a city lawn mower (definitely an oxymoron when thinking of lawn) would violently rape the dirt of its few and tightly held weeds. For a day or two, the courtyard hinted of order and pride. Those moments quickly passed. Any rain created little rivers meeting up into streams and headed for waterfalls from the closest curb.

We had an alley on one end of the project row. What a great place for tossing anything that would explode. Bottles were the grenade of choice, although rocks thrown against trash bins carried certain artillery-like echoes. There were some kids who played out back and, in the causeways, but most kept to the courtyards and streets. I've seen photos from network news stories showing some Middle Eastern country ravaged by conflict. There were streets that looked like some of our project alleys. I've thought, "Hey, that's 15th Place!"

ONE ALLEY WAS A SHORT DISTANCE FROM OUR BACK DOOR. Outside of most back doors there was the smelliest and most disgusting site: a garbage can. That's what was used instead of today's convenience of a garbage disposal. That miniature dented metal trashcan contained the waste scraped off plates for an entire week. You can imagine what else it contained toward the last few days of the week. Maggots and other gross creatures were all waiting to escape once the trashcan lid was opened. I wasn't a hefty or strong kid, but I managed to carry that trashcan at arms-length for the trek to the communal trash bin.

THERE WAS ONE EVENT THAT MADE IT WORTH BEING OUT BACK. I loved when the exterminators came to our neighborhood. I'm not talking about clearing out roaches and bugs, which was my very personal and specialized job. I'm talking about someone highly skilled in the art of rat extermination. It just so happens that Washington, D.C. employed such vermin specialists. They wore the same uniform as the guys who cut the dirt/grass or repaired pipes in the units—their tools branded for such a detailed undertaking. There were shovels, gloves, gas cans, and matches with usually two to four city workers surrounding a concrete bunker. Nothing mechanical or poisonous was necessary. The process was focused on one area for each unit, the back landing or concrete stoop. Rats could be seen at any time of day running under and from one stoop to the next. These were monstrous things for a kid.

The professional well practiced approach for those city workers was an effective six-step process. It went like this:

Step 1

Pour gasoline down holes on both sides of a given stoop.

Step 2

Position shovels in an upward menacing manner with feet and body braced for maximum downward thrust.

Step 3

Throw lit match into hole and watch flames blare out of both sides of stoop like fire-breathing dragon.

Step 4

Momentarily watch rats run out of holes.

Step 5

Beat the crap out of rats with shovel held by men who had feet and body positioned for maximum downward thrust.

Step 6

Collect dead rats with gloved hands.

The effectiveness of such endeavors was to be admired. Granted, the burnt-out infestations simply made room for new tenants.

IF THERE WAS PLAYTIME, IT WAS IN THE COURT AND NOT OUT BACK near the stoops. My younger sister liked the court because we could play outside without being out of sight of the front door or the classic yell of Mom calling us in for a TV dinner or—if we were unlucky—liver and onions.

I liked those aluminum foil covered meals mainly for the Apple Betty dessert and the chicken. I also liked mac-n-cheese and that very special yellow dye number 62 (or was its number 12). I never accepted that the peas were that bright green and that succotash was a part of any food group. Those lima beans probably could be found in the Old Testament as forbidden, along with hooved animals and pig snouts. At the time, I was certain that liver was a trick of the Devil.

Succotash was the one substance that was stored in my cheeks for as long as humanly possible. I vividly recall the marathon sessions at the kitchen table. Mom guaranteed we sat at the table until we had fully consumed every morsel, which, in many ways, didn't present a problem because I was always hungry. There were forces within me that welcomed certain foods (corn, chicken, potatoes, and all desserts).

Those same discerning taste buds also refused, with the utmost resistance, things such as the lima beans in succotash. I spent many evenings sitting at the table, amassing enormous amounts of saliva in my effort to resist swallowing even one lima bean. Given enough time, those green kidney-shaped things would decompose or hopefully, I would be abducted by aliens or lose consciousness. Unfortunately, they were trapped in my mouth without a passport to go further or permission to retrace their steps back to fork and back to plate. The inside of my growing cheeks became a human compost station. Inevitably, gravity and the mounting swell of saliva became too great, and the ugly act of swallowing followed. That vile vegetable medley never entered my mouth again once I left our court.

ALL THE COURTS LOOKED ALIKE BUT, IF POSSIBLE, SOME STOOD more dilapidated and destitute than others. To those passing by, thanking God they didn't end up on 15th Place—I'm sure every unit was equal in plight and despicableness. Actually, no one casually drove by unless they belonged. Today, I don't pass by any public-assisted housing without also uttering prayers of gratitude for making it out. I give a nod to those whose present day was my past. It takes an inmate of the neighborhood to appreciate the difference.

Many courts were on the low end of poverty. There are movies where innocent suburbanites make the wrong turn, finding themselves in an inhospitable place and easy prey. That was 15th Place to me and it was a mistake to enter or to linger.

The letter E configuration contained a total of twelve separate family units, which apparently was the brainchild of some city planner who lived far away. The design was used and reused until the human template became worn and unkempt. We all looked alike—Afros or nappy heads; noses and lips varying in size but always bigger and broader like JJ on the "Jeffersons". We didn't have any Lamont's from "Sanford and Son". The girls had nice big butts and the guys were lanky with slurred and faulty speech. They were all NBA wannabes. They took driving to the hoop very seriously. My look was not one of athletic material but more akin to be a seriously disinterested spectator sitting in the nose bleed seats reading a book or writing a story. I was born not interested in sports and not blending in.

Each dwelling within a court had its own front and back entrance without any signs of welcome. Doors were weathered, but not from years of exposure to harsh elements. Instead, entryways showed splintered wood, holes, and were primed with utter lack of care or concern. It was easy to understand the lack of ownership as I looked out across endless rows called homes. I never once aspired to or considered it successful to be master of my very own project home. Most tenants didn't either. Some children followed in the footsteps, which preserved and repeat the model—children begetting children begetting welfare checks. Habits are difficult to break if that's all one has ever known. Adequate education didn't lead to higher self-worth or expectations.

Photo of 15th Place and their projects.

Another photo of 15th Place, now destitute.

These inner-city fortresses were constructed of many materials simply wrapped or layered one upon the other. A new edifice was added as a result of yet another capital renovation campaign somehow wrangled out of city government funds. This process and new wrapping were issued every few years as if on cue.

I have trouble describing this image because the term renovation is something you hear in today's vernacular from television programs inspiring DIY projects and makeovers. In reality, many believed that D.C. was managed by a corrupt administration and misguided budget. So instead of removing and replacing, renewal involved putting one front on top of an already old front, which lay atop of yet another makeover. These in no way disguised or otherwise mislead one to believe it was anything but government-supported housing. It was instantly a new building but ancient and secure in its depressing landscape.

What's left of 15th Place in 2003.

Within that depressing landscape came certain expectations. I knew it wasn't safe or advisable to make direct eye contact with anyone except a few friends or unless I was well within the boundaries of my own court. One had to be skilled in the art of staring out of the corner of your eyes and therefore, not ever "looking". A quick almost imperceptible glance was the same as saying "hey!"—a social norm for the projects. Otherwise, a glance a second too long had the real potential for spawning cursing or fighting as if one's impoverished but protected territory was being threatened.

Many times, I witnessed through my corner vision, kids, adults, brothers, and sisters recklessly busting in and out of doors undeterred by lock or latch or parental limits if there were any. Residents sat on the stoop or hung out windows trying to detect a breeze during summers of exhausting heat and inescapable humidity. Foul language echoed back and forth like the last of a tribal dialect fighting to survive. I've yet to ever hear the ferocity and tenor of cussing (that's how it was described at the time) like that found up and down my 15th Place.

Now as an adult, project residents have little clue or care for my slow, periodic, and deliberate drive-by's. I was yet another black man and another stranger. On this last visit, I was shocked and became angry—just plain old pissed off with emotions. "It's all gone!" I shouted in my head, shuttering as if I were standing inside a ringing bell.

My crypt pried open and contents spilled out in disregard. It had vanished. A part of my life was evicted and scrapped. To be more accurate, the entire project, layers of roach-infested public housing, rats the size of gophers under every stoop, and those who menaced human kind were all gone, cleared away, and extricated. Every single brick and piece of wood in my 15th Place was bulldozed, shoveled up, and trucked away. Yeah, I was pissed off. My reaction was confusing.

Wait! Shouldn't there be cheerfulness? Even euphoria? I uttered aloud a few choice words well unbecoming of my maturity and station in life. It was ironic in a way that I was swearing as I look from the outside in when I couldn't muster those very same words when I was on the inside looking out.

Every visit to my former street in the projects was, in some way, an ascension to a holy place of victory. Subconsciously, when I drove by, stopped, stared, and became detached—a deep-seated guttural sound erupted into a mournful bellow that I had made it out of that god-forsaken place. When there was no court to see, to scream my victory at in my mind, I should have been overjoyed. Triumphant laughter should have filled the air.

Instead, there was a void that was inescapable. Those very same overwhelming feelings continue even now as I write.

How dare they attempt to wipe out that horrendous part of my memory, embossed as it is with deep-seated hurt down to my very constitution, my essence? No one asked my permission or allowed me appropriate time to mourn what would be lost. I was like one of those Chinese villagers being summarily removed from home after generations, simply to make way for a damned dam. It never dawned on me that one day, the landscape could or would change and erase years of self-contempt, cultural, and social embarrassment. Shouldn't this be considered unnecessary roughness, too?

I needed always to witness or to eye my nemesis. Merely seeing a window or doorway from a project building had a certain affect. Memories would always spill out in no particular order, returning thoughts, fears, senses— especially smells—without prompting. I knew the smell in the air of burning buildings and things that seemed precise to my 15th Place and the surrounding area.

I WAS MAD AT MY MOM FOR NOT LETTING US OUT OF THE HOUSE during the riots that followed the assassination of Dr. Martin Luther King, Jr. on April 4, 1968. I was eleven years old and could see smoke rising from looted and burning stores all about sixty seconds from the gates of the camp. Fire trucks and police cars raced back and forth with sirens blaring and lights flashing. I saw pieces of the action by peering out the back door or the upstairs bedroom window looking in between units. Even the National Guard sprung to life at Camp Simms. This was a first during the decade or so that we lived in 15th Place. Its fences bordered the backside of some of the stores. I thought it rather interesting that army soldiers were summoned. Convoys of military jeeps and trucks raced less than a block in order to guard stores that were already looted and burning. Those convoys were busy for the next few days as cars burned and protestors took to the streets.

Later after calmness settled back in, the after math of a collective people's despair and frustration with society was very evident. Unfortunately, the projects took it out on the projects. We torched, burned down and looted ourselves out of convenience stores, cleaners, liquor stores, and mom-and-pop grocery stores. I didn't fully appreciate the dynamics occurring between the "haves" and "have-nots" or black people and the rest of the world until I had opportunity to live outside the projects.

I assumed the rest of the world was one big project, too. What reason would I have to think differently until I ventured outside of its walls? I quickly appreciated one important fact. All of us in the projects had further to walk or to wait or to ride city transit buses to buy groceries and other goods after stores were looted and closed. I also knew a few in the projects that on one day had old stuff or no stuff, but the next day had new stuff and a bunch of it. Such was the "give and take" of life in my projects.

Sometimes I carve a jagged etching of gloom from my inner-city life. Yet, there were times of fun and play. Maybe it didn't fit the jungle gym or playground atmosphere of today. Kids will make the best use out of what they can.

4

PLAY TIME

"Play is often talked about as if it were a relief from serious learning. Play is really the work of childhood."

— FRED ROGERS

FRED ROGERS' QUOTE IS NOT EXACTLY MY LIFE'S STORY OR MY childhood. I was born into a state of "here and now" as with everyone who ever has been born. It's a state of good, bad, and a little in between.

Where were those times of in-between and of fun and play? My cheeks draw up, bringing out the crooked smile that takes hold when I think about some of those times of laughter and real child play. Honestly, I begged my subconscious to spill out something good and positive. I refused to accept that everything was a nightmare. I nearly forgot those moments of freedom and laughter existed.

Bike riding was my favorite past time. I didn't want to go outside but there wasn't always a choice as mom would force me out of the nest. "Fine," was my mumble as I stomped out of the back door to find my place on the stoop. Even that concrete sanctuary was short-lived as Mom would stick her head out the upstairs window to shout me off the step and away from the nest. When I had a bike, a daredevil adventure would brighten my world.

My bikes were classics of sorts. One had a sporty motorcycle style handle bar with tassels hanging from each end and a banana shaped seat. Like most classics, there was always some work to be done to maintain one's roadster. There were very few tools. So that meant riding a bike with handlebars that moved back and forth based on its own mood, the humidity, or day of the week. I'm thankful my seat was properly affixed because I needed the support when jamming my foot between tire and frame for braking. I was very adept at braking and only on occasion did my foot get wedged so tightly that upon stopping, I tilted and in slow motion, I fell over—creating my very own cloud of dust. I couldn't help but laugh aloud at myself despite the embarrassment.

I also had a serious old-style big wheel bike that was the eighteen-wheeler of bikes. It reminded me of an Electra or Easy Rider-style bike. My machine was sky blue with one peddle that constantly fell out. I wasn't discouraged by any mechanical problems but mastered the art of motoring along with just one pedal. I was skilled in catching the long medal arm that once housed the absent pedal—catching just at the right time at the top of each stroke. I would then ride the arm down a half revolution with foot readied for the next cycle. I could literally drag race down the street once the giant sprocket reached a constant rotation, a velocity unintended for a kid (or so it seemed). My Electra had one gear that strengthen calf muscles and tightened stomach muscles by the sheer force needed to propel the big rig. Again, brakes were inconsequential if my dime store PF Flyer knock-offs were not too worn out. It seemed like those tennis shoes would always reach that tattered state without much effort. I guess the true standard of pain and safety was whether the skin of my foot made contact with the rubber of the back tire. It wasn't difficult to manipulate around holes in my sole to apply breaking without losing footpad and skin.

Danger and fun came together and in different ways. Some might not consider smoking cigarettes —Kools —as part of the fun of childhood. There was a time when it was a dangerous and risky business that Bruce, Gerald and I did. It was fun in a very anxious sort of way. We first started taking puffs in our pretend adult world while in elementary school. It was cool. forbidden, bad which was quite uncharacteristic for us. Witnessing others in fourth, fifth, or sixth grade smoking on the way to and from school and sneaking a smoke during recess was not unusual. The three of us had our own covert way of getting our smoking time in.

We didn't pretend at hooky, we actually did it if only a few times. Snatching away to the woods across the street from Green Elementary School on Mississippi Avenue was like making our escape across the bay to San Francisco from Alcatraz and then returning unnoticed. We would go deep in the woods to avoid teacher's eyes always sniffing out trouble. That meant going deep enough into the woods until the elementary school building was out of sight. I don't recall who bought or stole cigarettes from his mother from one time or the next, but it sure wasn't me. My mother smoked even to a point of reacting like a drug addict when her stash was low or empty. Mom made no exception and would not allow any of us kids to smoke, despite her own nicotine habit. This was the taboo of taboos that didn't bear explanation. She barred us from smoking because "I said so".

In the woods we would light up and take long drags, releasing white smoke into the pristine air of our sanctuary. We waved clouds of smoke away just in case a teacher was lurking in the woods, searching for the many kids missing from school every day. We smoked those Kools one after the other until the school bell rang at 3:00 p.m. Sufficiently buzzed by cigarettes and stoked by breaking bad at age eight or so, we blended back into the school crowd rushing back up the street toward home. I was ready to become a steady user, an older bad kid finally fitting in to the crowd. I was cool and rebelling against myself. I was too terrified to be publicly defiant. Hey! My mother might find out and that might result in my execution.

One day, the unexpected occurred that quickly ended my quiet tobacco revolt. Mom found cigarettes. All hell broke out. Luckily, they were not my smokes since I wasn't insane enough to bring them into the house. Mom found them in the dresser drawer of one of my sisters. She waited for the female pirate to come home one afternoon. Once inside my sister was confronted with the "Captain Hook" of disciplinary action. My sister was drilled, questioned and walked to what I thought was the end of the plank—the end of life itself. However, I was wrong, it was much worse than death. Mom made my sister eat the cigarette. I didn't see the caustic event but the sounds of yelling, crying, and convulsions were shocking and more terrifying than any beating by bullies.

The consequence of being discovered far overwhelmed my desire to steel away for another drag. Gerald, Bruce and I stole away from elementary school a few other times, but I didn't smoke another cigarette even when we retreated to our wooded fortress. The power of Ms. Captain Hook was far reaching and controlled me even deep in the woods. The desire for the smooth, deeply satisfying taste of Kools stayed with me for many years but I never smoked again.

There were other less dangerous fun times. We didn't have Playstations or X-Boxes, but the level of concentration and expertise was equally intense and exhilarating. I was a kid during the Vietnam War so playing with my hundreds of plastic green soldiers was another one of my favorite past times. I would spend hours positioning soldiers around my room readied for battle. Play-by-play descriptions were articulated with strategy, executed, and recounted in the history book of my mind. There was certain attrition for my army men, which mainly happened when Mom or someone stepped on a forgotten soldier. You can imagine that soldier was immediately considered a casualty or KIA (killed in action).

Other pearls involved the ultimate and truly exciting game of "Dirt Bombs". I hated going outside because of the danger any soldier in any hostile territory would face. During the hot and humid summers, the ground would dry out and crack like the water-starved Serengeti of Africa. There born the ammunition for my game. Imagine taking one of those clumps of dirt and lobbing it into a village or pillbox. As the dirt bomb struck a wall or ground, a quiet explosion occurred. Contact could be seen from a distance because of the dirt cloud that followed a hit. Elementary school kids became the Special Forces, hiding behind buildings, trash bins and wrecked cars waiting to attack. Once an enemy was identified, a well-placed bomb could win the day. Cluster bombs (a handful of dirt bombs) or "Big Berthas" (large clump of dirt) were employed.

A successful mission occurred anytime one made a direct hit on an enemy. Granted, no enemy was ever killed or maimed. Never-theless, being struck by a dirt bomb was no fun and left a stinging impression. Sometimes, a worse encounter was had. I had such an occasion and became a war casualty that resulted in being rushed off to the field hospital.

I was fast, stealthy, and excellent at finding hiding places to launch attacks. Covertly running full out down one or two buildings was easy and usually gave me an advantage. I could lob a few bombs and track down to the next position before readying for another surprise offensive. I prepared to attack on one such move. As I leaned out from behind a three-story building across the street from my court, my eyes caught in slow motion a soldier's worse moment. I received a dirt bomb hit directly in the mouth. My enemy had improvised and threw a bomb with a rock embedded in it. The next moment found me bleeding profusely out of my mouth, blood running my dirtied neck and shirt. No longer a soldier but a kid, I ran home crying in pain to show Mom. Soldiers always ran home to their mom during emergencies. There were no dads to run home to. As Mom rushed me to the bathroom and tried to stop the bleeding, I could see in the mirror that my upper lip was split, my upper gums was deeply cut, and my front tooth was now slightly crooked—overlapping the other big tooth.

That's when Mom would say, *"To the hospital again!"*

Apparently, I made a habit of needing emergency room treatment. I wasn't awarded medals as a result of my injury. However, I did receive stitches to close my lip and a few stitches in my gums above my front teeth. As for the two big teeth, they still bear the outcome of that lost battle.

THERE WERE OTHER SKIRMISHES THAT WERE ALL TOO REAL, WHICH

occurred in the middle of fun. Grandma's house was the perfect playing field because it had a fenced in backyard with its own treasures worthy of defending. How many project kids had access to apples and pears in their own backyard? Where else besides the grocery store could you taste berries except off the vine or suck the sweet nectar of all the honey suckles one could manage except at Grandma's place?

Hers was the ultimate safe haven most of the time. Getting there without encountering more and new project bullies required a certain cunning. First, I had to navigate safe passage out of my own neighborhood.

It's interesting to think of the area as a neighborhood. That would suggest community, socializing, a sense of commonly agreed upon values. I couldn't or didn't want to believe that any of us wanted to be there and the brutality that existed made it impossible for me to accept there was a moral standard to be honored. I know now that even in the most difficult environments, many people of unfortunate circumstances have pride, contribute to society, desire better lives, are sympathetic, generous, and seek belonging and community. As a ten-year-old who always afraid and guarding his station in life—I certainly didn't appreciate that in my neighborhood.

Grandma's house wasn't in an idyllic part of southeast D.C., but it was certainly inviting boundaries beyond my world. Zigzagging through alleys and portions of less hazardous parts of the projects could deposit me safely on Stanton Road. I crossed Suitland Parkway and traveled past a long row of tightly packed eighty-plus-year-old houses. Imagine living in your own place, unattached from loud music, loud talk and loud living. It was the stuff of dreams.

Following this course carried me up and down a long curving

street. Ironically, as the street inclined downward so did the housing. Once again, I had to pass badlands to my left and right. Instead of several project dwellings connected to form the letter E like my 15th Place, these were four- or five-story buildings planted in dirt mounds towering over one another as the street graded to the bottom of the hill. There were occasional asks (not demands) for money from a wannabe thug I disregarded with a deeper than natural mumbled voice of "naw man," and kept walking to Grandma's house. I was always on alert. I would stop by the badlands to pick up my cousin Daryl. It was only then that my exaggerated project swagger could be relaxed. Daryl was big enough that he became my unintended bodyguard.

Occasionally, we were required to defend Grandma's yard from some really hardcore guys from Berry Farms. This was one of the few areas, through a patch of woods and across Suitland Parkway, which no one entered without being born into the very plight and anger of Berry Farms. This was the project of projects, ultimate and superior in its indifference and callousness. Guys from the Farms would raid the yard, targeting our fruit trees. Serious rock battles and fights took place of which Daryl was always the victor. My lefty hook was great for tagging them with a well-placed rock throw. I wasn't much good at throwing a punch. To this day, I'm certain Grandma's house wasn't vandalized like other homes on her street because those across the highway knew of Daryl.

As much as I love the fun of some of those battlegrounds, there was a certain non-combative peace found back in the woods. Mom would force me out of the house and there was nothing to do, which was most of the time. I would make my way down to the woods. Just stepping into the twist of trees, undergrowth, and brush presented suspense and mystery. I would seek this unknown out of curiosity and, in a way, as a private dare. I could push my uneasiness to the very edge but on my own terms and under my control. The woods didn't judge or much care who I was. It never pursued me in anger or some unknown reason, except that which my imagination allowed. My forest wasn't jealous and gained no value or satisfaction in reminding me of my designated place in society. I had a matter of fact agreement with my treed playground.

It said, *"you are welcomed. You can play."* And that was all. There were no other conditions.

I took advantage and became nearly fearless in my adventures. It was so unburdening not to be broad-nosed and oily-skinned in the summer heat of D.C. I wasn't black or white but just a kid who liked to feel his toes dipping in the creeks that snaked its way somewhere into the depths of the trees. The water was always cool—almost in defiance of the baking temperatures throughout the summer months.

Like Lewis and Clark, I mapped and traveled my territory. There was never any space for other little black boys from encasement. It must have been set aside as a preserve for Wendell since I never saw or heard another project kid breaking its silence with cursing and obnoxious laughter. Maybe they feared the one thing I bravely conquered.

I had an objective whenever the woods seemed to part and invite me in. I was an archeologist, a historian, a geologist, and a paleontologist all wrapped in one. My search was to discover the undiscovered. Maybe on that day, a rare coin would be found or some interesting rock. Maybe I would finally find a bullet up on Bullet Hill. Actually, that hill was more like a dirt mound holding up what was left of an ancient wall deep within the woods. Its location didn't make sense and was out of place, but it had a mystical sense about it. I didn't realize at the time how much Bullet Hill resembled my childhood life.

The wall had to be supported by a foundation, but I could never find it. I once started digging to uncover the base of the wall but quickly stopped. I realized the noise of my scavenging intruded loudly into the peaceful sounds of the forest. The trees, leaves bushes, crickets, and undergrowth protested by becoming completely silent. The absence of nature's sounds meant I would be abandoned and maybe barred if I persisted. I became still and blended back into nature—back into the woods—but continued a silent investigation. The disintegrating wall was made of stone or rock, much like houses from the Civil War era. The remaining wall had bullet holes pockmarked about it. Certainly, there was some untold history in this site deep in the woods. I never found spent ammunition, shell casings, or human bones to tell a story of war and death, although I searched desperately each time, I explored the wall.

I didn't venture past Bullet Hill deeper into the vastness of the woods. There was something a little spooky and unknown hidden in the thicket tangle of Mother Nature. My instincts, juvenile as they might have been, wouldn't allow me passage. If I couldn't handle the jungle-like existence in the projects, then how was I to survive that which blended into a darkness that forbad both sunlight and sound? Today, those enormous back woods are merely a track of land providing nature's backdrop for hundreds of homes in a nearby development.

As a kid, it was my personal playground, my Yellowstone National Park. In my memories, it still is that special quiet and fun time which granted reprieve from an unwanted day and life.

5

AISLE TWELVE AND MY AISLE TWELVE

"What's on the list?" I asked Mom in a mature and seasoned tone. There's a secret hidden for my entire life behind my question. She mused through hand written notes on a small piece of paper clipped with her ID and maybe a stamp or something. I know paper clips and safety pins have become part of her collective world of order, of list-making, and security against forgetfulness. Mom doesn't have any symptoms of dementia or memory loss. I've noticed similar over simplification and list making in other seniors, as if they are all prepared for the disease of forgetfulness.

The grocery list included among other things: powdered ranch salad dressing mix, extra-large biscuits, skim milk (for the granddaughter), and a box of eight Hostess Streusel caramel-covered cakes (as close to a spontaneous purchase as she gets for parent consumption). Mom has a sweet tooth that is obviously part of my DNA. We're beginning our journey through an unfamiliar grocery store as if sojourning in a new land. My task is to push the grocery cart.

My innocent secret hidden all my life was finally realized. I walked in a grocery store with my 75-year old mother as a male debutant—a coming out of sorts. I was grocery shopping with my mommy for the first time at the tender age of fifty-something. It was my time to maturely ride the grocery cart and eagerly find items on my mother's behalf. Maybe it's never too late for firsts.

A second and equally important goal was not to run over mom with the cart.

I gleefully maneuvered past stock boys and other mothers studiously examining packages at different angles searching for ingredients and caloric content. We searched for biscuits and gravy, whose fine taste comes from a cook's memory, through trial and tradition and not from cue cards or Internet recipes. Vanilla extract, real artery-clogging containers of lard, cinnamon, pineapple juice, and other secrets never written down but captured with the smell, look, and sight of the kitchen master— the grandma, the mother, the aunt or an occasional uncle who forgot his culinary place.

At one point, I launched a brief glide with both feet on the grocery cart when I knew mom wasn't looking and when it was clear of others rushing past to beat some invisible competitor to the twelve items or less line. This mother-and-son treasured excursion for me might be another child's arduous and unpopular nightmare. My own children always dreaded the grocery store visit as if they were called up for another arduous tour of duty in a distant desert on the other side of the world. Going up and down the aisles with mom was my first and only time we went grocery shopping together. Don't get me wrong, I did go to the grocery store as a kid and like every kid, I hated the abusive waste of time and muscle power.

My Aisle Twelve

I don't much recall going up and down food aisles as a kid. It was not a task to be enjoyed or require imagination or deviation. The list never contained stuff worth of eating in my estimation. I was a kid who was always hungry. Those infamous lists had my favorite items such as cereal, but it was never the kind I wanted or liked.

What we received was cereal which had bumps on it that made me feel ill every time I saw them. I ate those Apple Jacks and was left with cereal, which floated—bloated like a very tiny dead light brown seal. Then there was Wheat Puffs. It must have been manufactured specifically and only for those living in public housing. Those puffs were way too abundant in the grocery store. I can't believe anyone of a free and sound mind would willingly buy the inedible. There also were frozen blocks of vegetables retrieved from a nuclear mishap from the Cold War and sold as food stuff.

These uninteresting foods found their way to our place. I pulled a grocery cart made of stainless-steel bars crisscrossed in order to imprison paper bags bulging through every rectangular opening all balanced with two rubber wheels. The handle, always too short for a normal human being to walk upright, caused a noticeable slouch and an extra measure of droop from dejection and unsolicited pity. I always ended my shopping cart assignment with a bad back and a neck ache. My self-worth wasn't that much better off. The wheeled buggy was shiny, of course, so it could be seen blocks away and served as an appropriate signal of social and financial stature thus personal self-awareness and embarrassment.

Occasionally, I was able to ride my bike (when I had one, which was not very often) to pick up a few items from the five-and- or grocery store. Any bicycle was fair game for the taking but my ride had certain immunity. A bike was not rated as worth stealing when it was missing a seat, brakes, or had permanently-crooked handle bars. Riding a girl's bike wasn't an attractive option either. Even thieves had standards. I just needed something to get me there and back.

The rider, however, was entitled to all rights and privileges acceded to the weak and nerdy. Translation—I was granted entry into the store—money intact, but my exit included passing any change to whomever said "hey, give me your money". Sometimes there was an expectation of fists in the face if the passionless statement were not obeyed. I appreciated the respect afforded my mother in that I could enter the store with money intact. Bags were never rifled through or items taken. Again, I think an example of an unspoken creed amongst thieves and thugs. There was hope that society hadn't completely been abandoned in chaos and survival of the fittest. Anyway, I don't think my adversaries carried can openers, bowls, and the like for quick meals.

Regardless of the mode of transportation, I would scope out the likely impending confrontation. How many guys were staged outside and around the corner of the store? One couldn't enter the store that was within a five-minute walk of home without passing them and without them assessing whether an easy mark was at hand. The more guys out front meant there was a greater chance of being harassed or hit. I understand the phrase "misery loves company" or "urban warfare." Frankly, there wasn't anything else for these guys to do but to hang out and take from those who had nothing to give.

My own ability to observe, analyze a situation, and derive

options developed early as a result. We nerds had this natural talent. I tried walking with a cool lean, a swagger, and a heavy pimp—wearing the face of a hardened underprivileged minority. There were no points for style or showmanship. Once identified as a nerd or a ghetto geek, always a nerd or a ghetto geek. There were times when the risk was so overwhelming, due to the cast of characters waiting, that I decided it best to go to another grocery store across state lines. At least it felt that way.

There was no money to take city buses so every leave from base camp (home) was by way of overly worn tennis shoes with holes, allowing feet or toes to make contact with bare concrete in every stride. That made for a sloshy existence on rainy or snowy days. It was well within my means to take a circuitous route that added two and a half miles one way to my usual couple hundred yards. I knew how to avoid mine fields when necessary. It was easier to face the ire of Mom for taking too long to return from the store than encounter the wrath of an enemy without anything else to do. It was from these and other episodes that my stride and endurance grew into my being a pretty good long-distance walker and cross-country runner in school. Go figure!

WE FINALLY MOVED FROM 15ᵀᴴ PLACE BY THE TIME I BEGAN HIGH school. I became a real-life JJ borrowing the 1970s theme song "Movin' on Up." We moved to the third floor of an apartment building two and a half miles from school and about one mile from my confinement of some nine years. I was overjoyed with my release even knowing misery hadn't been freed altogether. Going to high school would mean going directly through the gauntlet twice a day five days a week. I took point every day for a unit of one. Certain tactics were deployed to increase odds of ongoing survival. I could see far enough ahead of my walking trip to school making it possible to quickly assess options. Should I assume a hard ass walk hoping to grant passage across the grocery store front with guys still attached to the outside wall? I wonder if they worked in clocked time cards, or if there were a gentleman's agreement as to time and ownership of the corner store. The corner of the store was always occupied.

Sometimes my overly animated gait was the ticket to temporary freedom and access to nondescript groceries. There were other occasions where the store wall inhabitants amassed as if waiting for transportation to the nearest farm fields for another hard day in the sun. Unfortunately, I could never master the read in zombie like expressions when my i'm-like-you-walk would grant a nod, thus passage through the malaise. On other instances, I would circle far out arching left around the throng of guys, the strip stores and about half the neighborhood. The route gave way to a richer and safer valley below. Taking a similar circumventing course to the right would skirt dangerous territory near the infamous Johnson Junior High School. Surely that was a dumb man's attempt at suicide. As usual, circling to the left would add an additional twenty minutes or so to my destination but by now my legs were strong and my mind well prepared to reach the safe ground of high school.

Once there, I was free to be me without repercussions for "nerdiness", and for being inquisitive and intelligent. Flaunting these growing characteristics required ego which was never my thing. I wasn't certain how long my mind could keep up this act—this trick of learning and retaining stuff. Maybe I wasn't a geek after all. Well, that might be going too far. Even teachers invited me to explore this new world. Finally, self-discovery grew in a bright sanctuary granted during most high school days.

6

I AIN'T ON NO WALLS

I FORGET THE CIRCUMSTANCES THAT LED ME TO HAPPEN UPON THE only family picture of mom, my brother, and three sisters. In this photo, I was a child. The photo was new to me. It was the only family picture I had ever seen and the only one of me as a child. I looked handsome as a three-year-old with a head shaped like an alphabet block from Mattel. Placed in a quaint distressed gold picture frame laced with a string of pearls over one corner, it became the look that lent itself to a family history. When in actuality, there I was, out of nowhere.

People are born, and they are delivered into the world as the starting point in life. The very first photos would show welcoming smiles, and relatives crowded around marvelling in the darlingness of a new birth. Babies receive instinctively warmth and love and kept completely protected from hardship or danger. My memory, the start of childhood, began at one harsh point. It seems my life was simply instigated, if you will, somewhere about the age of elementary school. I realize it makes sense that most memories can be retrieved from about ages four or five. In and of itself, my start is not unlike others. I just don't like the jumping off point of my memory. I would have hoped for happier beginnings. I would have gone for a "do over" if offered.

I didn't notice the absence of my pictorial self until much later in life. It's still strangely out of the ordinary and curious not to have existed until a certain point. Oh sure—my aunts kept stacks of photo albums and boxes of pictures of every family gathering and activity. They are the living versions of hoarders with boxes, cubbyholes, and hidden books of pictures turned yellow with antiquity. Thank goodness for them.

Every box held its version of black and white freezes of relatives as part of a very old family tree. I have great- and great-great uncles and aunts, and cousins four and five times removed on my grandfather's brother's side. I think somehow everyone in the world is related to me. I'm told this is your aunt whomever by way of lines connecting back to someone standing beside what appears to be 1920s Ford cruiser. I study each faded and crinkled photo and pages of unknown people as if I were a crime scene investigator hoping to discover hidden signs enabling me to reconstruct who I am.

They were proud people, claiming their existence. I often wondered why these still photos never seemed to capture anyone smiling or appearing to be happy, as if it were against photo etiquette to demonstrate joy and gaiety. As I recorded each character and portrait, our blackness was the only similarity that tied us together. Otherwise, I didn't look like them and they were strangers to me. Color photos were usually at the top of the piles. They showed more contemporary times such as last week's Fourth of July gathering, graduation parties, retirements, and the like.

Our sole family picture was in the black and white that I

temporarily borrowed from a relative. Its aged appearance helped to qualify a point and time in my life. The colored pictures showed me as a young teenager, capturing my grin and frozen laughter shining bright with cousins, nieces, and everyone else considered family. Kids are always camera hams posing in that casual and spontaneous yet contrived way.

Mom did not have family photos framed and mounted on walls or shelves, showing off a neat and polite looking brood of five. Come to think of it—she didn't have any baby pictures anywhere. Therefore, I don't have baby pictures to share. How am I to bequeath that which reflected my life as an infant? What is there to pass on showing my contentment and security as a baby? Where is the picturing of my months and years of growth to finally becoming the man that I am today? I would have to make it up if not for the photos held by a few aunts—the family historians. There weren't any photos of Mom with the girls or ok-stay-where-you-are   mom-boys-come-stand-by-her-side polaroids. It was as if Mom was part of a witness protection program, erasing photographic evidence of a family to protect the life and innocence of someone.

Our family reminded me of an old movie whose title has long been forgotten. In pasts unknown, intrusive neighbors dug for clues. Long story short, it was the buzz and near hysteria that only a small town can create about the well-schooled and well-mannered man. He was supposedly an alien—not from across the border but some place in the cosmos. Maybe I, too, was born from a similar distant place only to be situated in the southeast part of the District of Columbia. The goal was to blend in, observe, and record life on this bizarre planet. This alien was ill-prepared to blend in.

Mom often said she didn't like having her picture taken. Perhaps it was more believable that the lack of family photos has a deeper meaning. Mom's dismissive statement is but a convenient means for deflecting something greater, something deeper, or some kind of hurt she didn't want to relive. I believe Mom had what I would call the "dark years" when we lived or survived the daily life, in public housing.

Even to this day, my mother is skillful at evading digital and video cameras. I've resorted to "drive-by photos" with a slight twist of paparazzi talent. This involves a casual walk by and quickly snapping a shot from camera partially hidden under my armpit or low at hip level. My gait was steady and never slowed as I aimed for that invisible destination across the room. Most times, I end up in a near desperate run, as if a fugitive son escaping the irritated grabs of his mother's hands, spurred solely by the slight perceptible clicking sound of the camera. Manufacturing a mafia hit man like silencer for cameras can be the next best invention. Mom is light on her feet and her "get up and go" is surprising at times for a mother of eighty-something. There was a time or two when she chased after me when a camera flash caught her attention. I would laugh nervously as my stride kept me just out of reach of her pinching fingers.

Much like the pictorial absence of my mother, I never saw a photo of my father with any of us kids or of his bride. What might that day of matrimony have been like? Were they welcomed down aisles sided by wooden pews planted firmly in burgundy carpet surrounding the sacred alter of a church? As they made their way past generations of kin folk, maybe they walked in sync to traditional wedding music. Perhaps the ceremony itself introduced family to lovers and lifelong commitment, of cherished memories and family. A dream—perhaps—but one would have wanted so badly for my mother.

The real life to follow was anything but matrimonial bliss. I feel somehow responsible for the life to follow. I've gathered much from the careful and halted words of my sisters. How could anyone get away with treating my mother with a casual disregard and contempt? She was certainly the matriarch with a heavy stern voice and a heavier hand. I couldn't imagine anyone —husband, dad or friend—surviving the veracity and fire that sometimes burned with fear in my little heart when mom meant what she said.

There were many times when I could honestly say I feared my mother. This was during her "dark period" which happened to be my period of "unnecessary roughness". The risk of encountering corporal and group punishment was high, especially throughout the summer months. We were home with nothing to do and chores didn't rank as fun, interesting or inspirational. We were motivated on several occasions with the idea of completing all household assignments within about two minutes. That occurred when someone happened to spot mom coming home sooner than expected from work. We were never successful our race to complete assignments before mom made it through the front door.

Sometimes Mom seemed to have an extra level of mad intensity making for quite a ruckus when you think about at least three kids getting spankings. Who would get it first and bear the brunt for the others? Those spankings, which we called whippings, were more earned by my crazed sisters due to their devious and bodacious actions. Witnessing those titan encounters, I was motivated to stay more between the lines by keeping the bad things out of sight. Admittedly, I veered across the line and into oncoming traffic a few times but luckily mom never found out about my not so angelic ways. Hey, even the best sibling has or should have a secret or two.

That was mom. What about a dad and a father figure? From what I could remember as a child, Dad was this man of such height and broadness that a person could completely disappear behind his manliness. His voice resonated with a thickness and intimidation emanating from a chest that was best described as thick and meaty like a sturdy large book found standing proudly on the last shelf of a library. He was dusty, and his mere presence commanded a certain awe-inspired pause as one reads the large calligraphic print of the man he was. Granted, I was a little kid looking up to what seemed to be a giant. I also acknowledge some of these imagines may be more of a wanted and hoped for a "dad persona" this project kid really wanted and desperately needed. It was verses imprints left from the real live hero every child deserves.

Ironically, I found myself staring one day at photos of his life. They consisted of family, friends, trips and visits all frozen in moments of laughter and connection. I stubbornly resisted the thought that they were signs of a happy existence. I couldn't escape the overwhelming sense of a fissure or gap in the DNA of our family string. The real problem was the absence of these" polaroid moments" showing me, un my inhibited sisters, or a scholarly brother endeared with family and friends. Those photos were of many strangers that seemed part of a lengthy act in an unrated European film badly portraying innocence and connectedness. For us, a subplot played in a language without subtext to understand. If the play was presented at the RKO Theatre in northwest Washington, D.C., it would be the across-town show we could not find enough bus tokens and transfer tickets to attend, criticize, or participate in. These people knew dad but didn't know the other side of the man. They did not recognize me, or the southeast family abandoned by its patriarch. How could they be linked with the man who gave me in part my baritone voice, broad nose, and a spirit of kindness without being aware of the real family? Even to this day, after having known some, I find a certain curiosity in scenes of family, as if fabricated and inserted into life. I'm probably related to most but never quite felt as though I am part of the inheritance. I've come to understand—but not accept—the deep-seated revulsion a few of my siblings had for Dad.

Dad didn't participate in developing my life. However, he came back into the reel of film of my life during my sophomore year at college. Now, I have pictures of him. There are even a few photos of us together. I still wish there was a sense of belonging and thus genuineness reflected in those still life images.

7

TODAY IS FRIDAY, AND MY FATHER IS DYING

I SHARE A FEW DIFFICULT MEMORIES OF MY FATHER THROUGHOUT THE book. Although they are few, those recollections are very intense and personal. My dad reentered my life when I was in college and we developed this quasi-father-and-son relationship. loved him but wasn't sure why. He turned out to be a very good man. In a maniacal way, I had hoped for a man I could loath. I had reasons to be angry and unforgiving. I was always quietly blaming Dad for Mom's hard life— secretly accusing him of my misfit place in this world.

My father was dying at the age of seventy-nine. I was fifty-six years old but at times, I feel the emotional confusion of a twelve-year-old wanting to play with his dad. I don't quite know what to do with all these feelings. Somehow, it felt right to add this now and present story to the then and past reflected in this memoir. They are uniquely coupled.

~

I MET MY DAD YESTERDAY IN A HOSPITAL BED ON THE FIRST FLOOR of a hospice facility. He is dying. Today is Friday.

I've been to emergency rooms and intensive care units. Those familiar and expected sounds were absent on this Friday. People weren't rushing in and out securing bags of blood, x-rays, or other vital measures. There were no sounds I've come to associate with life-and-death situations at least according to dramas normally found on prime-time television. Conspicuously absent were doctors with arrogant personalities rushing through trauma doors with medical personnel clamoring atop a body in cardiac arrest. The familiar hisses, clicks, and rhythmic sounds of an emergency room weren't echoing beats of a mechanical environment staged at the ready with oxygen or instruments under a chaotic lifesaving orchestration. I didn't see loved ones and friends frantic with fear, hyperventilating at the thought of death that was so imminent yet so anticipated.

My father's air and surroundings of death lingered in a temporary residence of a hospice facility. Though more like a quaint cottage found on the way to autumn in New England. This was more of a respite, a brief stop on the way to a needed vacation setting.

TODAY IS FRIDAY, AND MY FATHER IS DYING.

I had talked to my stepmother the week before in response to an email announcing another hospitalization for dad. Her words were kind and delicate yet hauntingly accepting of a fate that was years in the making. She never said my father was dying—perhaps this was her way of not completely rejecting hope or succumbing to the idea that there would be no miracle today. Softly, she said that Dad was in the end stage of Alzheimer's disease. I listened with an unanticipated indifference. The robbing of my dad's mental capacity—maybe better described as the mental implosion of his brain—began well before my Friday visit to his hospice room. I knew the insidiousness of Alzheimer's began several years ago, scouting out paths of destruction. Dad's deterioration had become evident about five years ago.

What should I feel? What should I say in response to my step-mother's hesitant announcement? I'm fifty-six years old and my father is dying. I promised that I would come and see Dad soon.

It might be apparent at this point that mine is not a story of an adopted child finding his parent all too late. However, a twist of that very scheme played out in my life.

I've known of and eventually knew my father and his sweet and committed wife of twenty years. Nevertheless, in many ways, I haven't known my father for most of my life. So, at the halfway point of my life it had finally come to this. The hopeful boy in me may have arrived at hospice on that Friday to die unwanted as well.

A certain image comes to mind when I consider my relationship with my father. I'm the kid pressing his face through criss-crossed bars—hands gripping tightly to cool rusted steel, hoping to break free from a space confined by time and inten-tional forgetfulness. I visited Dad several times during the past thirty years. He saw my family grow up a day here and there over those same decades.

During each visit, I peered through those bars, shouting my boyish heart's dream to regain and to live anew a mislaid part of my life. Surely it was meant for me but inexplicably misplaced like keys to a car or a favorite pair of leather gloves. It seems car keys are always found eventually but gloves are more easily dismissed with a resignation that they can be replaced. I felt like those worn and creased gloves situated in the back of the closet. I'm here—only if Dad would simply look behind the scarfs, hats, and sweaters worn by his other family. I just want him to check the back of the closet of his heart. I can't replace him like gloves.

With each visit from Dad, my lips moved frantically—speaking thunderous volumes as my eyes passionately searched his for whispers of regret and acknowledgement. My reality, however, donned a familiar persona of a quiet and respectful son who greeted his dad with hugs and amused him with the latest antics of his five grandsons. I longed for my invisible years to be returned like a holiday present given without a tear or wrinkle in the wrapping paper. I sought even the joy of a bow so perfectly affixed to my present but it, too, was stolen well before every Christmas morning throughout my childhood.

Today is Friday, and my father is dying.

Conversations were respectfully tempered at the hospice home. It's ironic to think of it as a home although it would end up being his last living place. It was the same muted dialogue found in a jewelry store where people admire diamonds. An air of culture, maturity, and calmness must be maintained when viewing exquisite stones through a jeweler's glass caseor a body and mind in decay in a hospice bed. Visitors walked by my father's room and to the bedside of another mother, father, or someone else. Smiles are interestingly plentiful and the banter at the coffee dispenser are almost ordained as part of the dying ritual. Most who ushered by were Caucasian with a few African-Americans. Those who are dying are of the same race in a way since death ultimately has no distinguishing characteristics. We all will die.

I flew into town on Friday morning and saw my dad by mid-day. It was only having seen his body, exhausted of the muscle and fat that defined his strong presence. I connect the words of finality so softly spoken by my stepmother. They were words of inevitability, surrendering to the act the disease prescribes.

TODAY IS FRIDAY, AND MY FATHER IS DYING.

Dad has always been this bigger than life figure to me. I met him for the first time as a baby but my memory of him started as a sophomore in college. I forget the circumstances leading up to that meeting, but it felt reassuring but strange to meet the man who contributed to my existence. Dad offered some dollars here and there during those college years but nothing to pay for the tuition, the apartment, or for anything substantial. I don't think I was looking for that anyway, although I feel it would have been a gesture of contrition. Maybe I wanted this. Or maybe I wanted an explanation—more than money could satisfy.

Dad would, on occasion, proudly exclaim to others my college and career accomplishments. It was always an uneasy feeling in that he received praise for raising a fine boy. Actually, it would make me angry as any accolades belonged exclusively to my mother and me. It wasn't fair that my dad received honor simply by association. I always carry this within me even to this day. I would call Dad on Father's Day only after having called my mom to give her first rights to credit and pride. I would call mom first for any huge milestone. Most of the time, I wouldn't share those occasions with Dad at all. It was my way of secretly carrying my anger and giving my mother recognition for that which my father refused to or couldn't commit to.

Today is Friday, and my father is dying.

WE STARTED OFF FOR THE HOSPICE FACILITY, DRIVING DOWN highways leading from one side of town to the other. A major metropolitan city gives little break to the anxiousness of a day of dying. The long drive across town trailing my stepmother and her daughter was harrowing in and of itself. No GPS system could have guided me through the many turns and sudden jaunts from far-left to far-right lanes and exits. Everyone was on the road in the middle of a workday. Surely, not that many people were in hospices with family coursing through town toward a final dying place.

I escorted my stepmother into a building with walls painted spring yellow. The hospice home was tucked between commercial businesses and office buildings surrounded by an explosion of greenery from trees and plants. It was rather ironic that plantings were anxiously awaiting Mother Nature's approval to begin life while encasing a place waiting for death.

Dad's room was the first one down a short hallway and to the right. As we stepped into this single occupancy room, there in the middle was my father. He was stretched out and listless. No matter. My stepmother assumed her normal and instinctive role of loving wife. She was drawn to him by unseen forces which summoned her eyes and touch to his face as if it were the day after their marriage ceremony.

"Open your pearly whites," she lovingly demanded with a warm laugh.

She repeated this several times with each attempt arching louder in hopes of penetrating his mental malady. Her hands cradled his white whiskered face. "You were shaved yesterday but not today," she said.

Dad's facial hair was course in that manly fashion. Hair grew in his nose and ears in that unkempt look as well. He was alienated from himself.

Despite my years of pent up questions, hidden anger, and uncertain feelings—I found myself in an instinctive state of son-to-father reaction. Without considering my approach or thoughts, I started speaking to my dad as if we had been close all my life. A sympathetic and gentle "hello Dad" emanated from my mouth without permission. My hands reached out, touching and stroking his without pensiveness. I lightly felt his thin plantings of white hair and looked deeply into the thinly open slits in his eyelids. Who instructed my brain synapsis to fire off these instructions? I was being the faithful son who, in some way, was grateful for having a father—a dad. I didn't seem to have control over my actions on that day.

How should I feel? What should I feel?

Honestly, I had no idea what the correct or appropriate sentiment should be. There were no tears as I didn't feel that within. Perhaps streams could have been running down my cheeks. I could have spoken with a voice wavering and cracking on the verge of losing emotion control? Was I fighting back a reaction or trying to conjure up some kind of sensitivity that a son ought to emote? I was very confused inside but outwardly—my actions were those of a loving son supporting a loving father.

As my stepmother stroked Dad's chest. It was evident how diminutive he became. His chest was still mighty like a barrel with steel strappings. But it also had the look of being hollowed out and slowly caving in on itself. His shoulder blades protruded in defiance and his long thick fingers reflexed to his face at times in a lost exercise without a purpose. Part of his left leg and knee lay uncovered to reveal a long vertical scare from a knee replacement years ago. Those knees and now skinny legs stopped working well before their time.

Through the sound of his beloved's words, Dad stirred ever so slightly as if to say, "I know you're here." If only he was able to acknowledge for a brief moment before retreating back into himself. His eyes never opened fully and what few times they managed to open, they showed a man lost behind distant clouds. Dad slept our entire visit, which was very much his daily routine for many weeks. At one point prior to being moved to hospice, he had slept for over five days without waking up. I believe his mind was forgetting to remind him of the daily routine of living.

We stayed with Dad for two or three hours. It may have been shorter given he slept through our visit. My stepmother sat on one side of dad's bed and I on the other side. She talked about his family and his eight siblings. This was a total surprise to me. I had met six of them on a handful of occasions. How is it that a son had never heard of an additional uncle and aunt who were long deceased? I never knew that Dad left home and moved in with his grandmother at age sixteen because his siblings would regularly abuse and beat him. I lived with his parents for two months just after marrying my eighteen-year old wife when I was twenty-one. Dad's grandfather and three of his siblings had Alzheimer's while most had high blood pressure, diabetes, or both.

"Just great," I mumbled in defeat.

I have hypertension, type I diabetes, and high cholesterol. I keep an eye on my brother who is four years older than me for any early signs of the brain disease.

"Damn it! Just great!"

TODAY IS FRIDAY, AND MY FATHER IS DYING.

Did my father treat my mother so badly due to his upbringing and experience with his siblings? Did mean brothers and sisters drum a horrible behavior into his life during the early part of his life? I was curious about the possibilities to an explanation for my life. I was equally disturbed at the prospect of the truth. Dad served nine years in the Air Force and eleven years in the Army. I learned more about my dad on his deathbed then I had in the preceding fifty years.

My father's Alzheimer's life began many years ago, but an event accelerated his symptoms and disease. I received a text one day about two years prior to his death. My stepmother shared that Dad had been hospitalized for several days. He had awakened feeling hungry one night at home and searched for something to eat. In the morning, my stepmother found him on the kitchen floor, unconscious. It was never determined how long Dad was laid out on that cold floor. He apparently had opened a kitchen cabinet, and something fell out. Dad bent to retrieve the item and severely struck his head while rising back up.

During his stay, it became apparent that Dad was experiencing dementia, DTs, or alcohol withdrawal symptoms. I had once heard that dad had always enjoyed his drinks, although I never knew exactly what or how much he consumed. I later found that his wife would hide or remove alcohol in the house. But he seemed to find a way to maintain his dangerous addiction. His drinking pattern even dated back to the time with Mom and my siblings. Dad was already in the throngs of dementia and Alzheimer's but the head injury and ensuing attempt at detoxification amplified the extent of his mental disease.

I went back to the hotel that night uncertain about today's feelings and what to expect the next day. I didn't want to think any more, so I went to bed around 8:30 pm. As I lay in bed in the dark, I realized the extent of my inner turmoil. I was exhausted, and by morning, that feeling hadn't dissipated despite sleeping some twelve hours. Mental and emotional distress always has a greater toll on me than any exercise regimen.

TODAY IS FRIDAY, AND MY FATHER IS DYING.

My emotional composure was swinging about wildly—not certain which direction the pendulum should swing. I question whether it would ever find a natural resting point at dead center. As I drafted my thoughts about Dad for this chapter, a childlike poem flooded my mind. Desperately, I captured every rhyme and verse fearful that expressions would quickly withdraw back into my mental vault housing emotional hurts and damage. It was truly simply a matter of capturing that which spewed without invitation. Therefore, I ask that you look beyond juvenile verse to understand my inescapable vacuum:

I once was lost
Not sure could be found
Lived in the projects
Hit and knocked around

Little and nerdy

Bookish like so
Made fun of and mocked
This boy couldn't grow

Where is my father?
Nowhere to be found?
What was it about me?
He couldn't stick around?
I studied, I learned
I ran and hid
Every punk was
Waiting
To pounce on
This ugly kid

Where did he go?
Was a dad ever there?
Must have been present
Wasn't born in the air!

Mom struggled
A harsh life indeed
Five kids to feed
Always hungry
I wanted more
Was my creed

Want more shoes
One pair this year
Rain and snow

I'll do alone
Not fair and right

Keep out of anger
Angry as I might
I'll become a man
Without a father's light

Old and accomplished
Five boys a legacy
Still a kid, a boy
Searching for
His infinite destiny

Where is my father?
Nowhere to be found
What was it about me?
He couldn't stick around?

— "The Lost Boy"

Today is Saturday, and my father is dying.

We arrived again from across town through traffic and rain that seemed like another bustling rush hour during the week. Dad was asleep again, but my stepmother had asked that he be repositioned because of bedsores. As we moved him, he uttered a man's weaken shriek of obvious pain. During Dad's last hospitalization, doctors were unable to determine the source of pain emanating from his leg. He couldn't talk or otherwise convey when he was in discomfort other than moaning when moved around in his bed. I didn't like knowing, especially hearing my father's painful demise.

I also didn't understand why I was bothered with this fact.

Shouldn't I sense something deeper and soulful other than a generalized feeling of sympathy for anyone in pain? Where was my empathy? He was both anyone and my father, but it was a wrestling match to unknot the two giving greater weight to the father side of the equation. Which one wins the match? I've yet to determine an outcome.

Today is Saturday, and my father is dying.

Today, it was time to see if Dad would eat. He hadn't eaten the day before and maybe the last few days. He did receive fluids to reverse the effects of dehydration. The assistant brought in a tray of colored blobs looking more like something found on a painter's pallet. His food consisted of pureed carrots, peas, meat and gravy without seasonings. It was baby food. Dad was fed a little at a time because when he did eat, his mind didn't remind him to swallow so his pureed food just sat inside his deflated cheeks. I wouldn't really describe it as eating but rather more a process of partial mechanical chewing.

Dad's bed was raised to an upright position. He lay somewhat awkwardly to his left like someone leaning in a car as it careens around a corner. I was told this was the result of a second stroke on the same side as his initial stroke. It was diagnosed during Dad's last hospitalization. The assistant eventually adjusted his head on the pillow to straighten his position and present a more normal look for someone in the state of dying. To our surprise, Dad ate his puddles of colorful foods although I'm still uncertain that his eyes ever opened.

I left Dad that Saturday somewhat encouraged by his eating. But I knew he would not survive much longer. I kissed his head and spoke in a strong sturdy voice, telling Dad I loved him. I had said and meant those words whenever we talked. They indeed were said with genuineness, although the feelings usually married to them were often absent. Sunday morning, I returned on a flight home and my dad was still dying.

TODAY IS TUESDAY, AND MY FATHER IS DEAD.

I took a flight on Monday for a business trip and on Tuesday morning, I received a call from my brother. Dad had passed. Our exchange was brief and oddly, my tone was appropriately regretful. How do I describe my feelings? I had none. I went through the entire day attending a business conference. I joked and chatted with others. I jotted relevant notes from speakers. I considered the application of principles in my work environment.

When I wasn't occupied with facts from keynote speakers, my mind pondered the whys of my lack of emotion. I still wasn't able to find answers or explanations. I sat through breakout sessions and more speakers but honestly, I don't recall anything that was said. I had fewer notes and then none at all. I eventually found my eyes looking down in my lap as if I were a bird perching over a cliff searching for prey. I never made it to the company dinner that evening. I could no longer maintain the guise of interest and polite conversations as if everything in my world remained unaffected and unchanged.

Later, my brother called on behalf of my stepmother asking if I would be a pallbearer. I agreed only if my brother promised to be one as well and that he wouldn't back out at the last minute. I didn't feel that I could be the only child out of four (one had passed away) from his loins appearing to be the loving son in mourning. What my insistence truly spoke of was my discomfort and unwillingness to be used when I was never part of Dad's family. It seemed like a charade and embarrassment that I was secretly sworn to an oath never to utter or betray.

The wake or viewing was on the following Tuesday. I was relieved when my brother suggested not attending since we all arrived in town late and tired. I never liked the idea of having the last image of someone from a coffin. The funeral was the next day. As we proceeded down and around church pews toward the open coffin, I assessed my feelings. Once again, my mind and body seemed to be devoid of them. I approached the coffin and thought for once someone looked good in their coffin.

Oh yeah. That was my dad.

Well, so much for not allowing a viewing to be the last mental image. I had to make the hushed processional journey moving a few steps at a time. The line of smartly dressed mourners moved along like we were making our way to a border crossing to be searched. Traffic was orderly, and we had no other direction to move but forward and pass the crossing of the coffin. The funeral home did a good job of presenting the man that everyone else had come to know, admire and love.

I didn't touch Dad or the coffin but I stopped and gazed uttering the words,

"Okay, Dad."

I'm not sure why those words were chosen or what they were intended to convey. Later, I thought and believed those two words were meant as a final point of forgiveness. Okay, Dad! You didn't acknowledge your wrong and ask for forgiveness directly. However, lived your life as a good husband and Christian man. Okay, Dad! I forgive you.

As I stood in front of my assigned seat, my stepmother of twenty years approached the coffin. She cried and leaned heavily on two family members helping her to stand. It was then that tears ran down my cheeks. I wiped them away only for more to follow. I quickly realized that my tears were for the loss my stepmother was experiencing. She lost her sweet love. I wasn't crying for my loss but for the separation my stepmother would now endure. My brother and others spoke of how well Dad honored and took care of his wife, served the church, and was a comic. He always lightened the mood and made everyone feel welcomed. It didn't seem real to me.

TODAY IS WEDNESDAY, AND MY FATHER IS DEAD.

From the church, we went to the cemetery, where Dad had a military gun salute. A bugler played "A Lost Solder" and the American flag was presented to his widow. We then proceeded back to the church where conversations, laughter, and food were had. Pages of countless photo albums were flipped through amongst the sounds and banter of a joyous family reunion. I was laughing and talking along with everyone else.

That atmosphere subtly changed for me as I viewed one photo album after another. As I listened to several who said I looked and sounded "just like my Dad", it dawned on me that I was nowhere to be found in those albums except for the baby pictures Dad received over the years. I was reminded of my disconnection and detachment from the world that was Dad's family—part of the good man spoken about at his funeral. Resentment bubbled to the surface at the idea that I was my father's son. I had his deep distinctive and heavy sounding core. I asked others if my sisters or brother resembled Dad more—not so much as a potential point of fact but more of a hope.

It was very important to me that I did not look or sound like my dad. It wasn't fair to Mom or to me. I didn't want to become unresponsive and in an eternal state of sleep at age seventy-nine. I wanted desperately to avoid becoming lethargic and mentally depressed as he did in his hospice bed. His dad—my grandfather—and two of Dad's brothers plus one sister had the "disease". Therefore, it seemed very logical that the more I favored and sounded like Dad, then maybe I would also be destined for his inevitableness. This was my attempt to otherwise minimize the chance of also inheriting my dad's Alzheimer's when he didn't leave me anything else to claim or cherish.

I'm too old to be living in such a complex emotional and mental state. I have forgiven my father and now must learn to live with what I have and didn't have.

I also now have a greater appreciation of the true value of being there for my boys, even though I am divorced from their mom. I so desperately want to ensure a pattern that haunted my life is finally and completely out of the closet. It will never become a dreadful experience in my children's lives.

Today is Wednesday, and my father is dead.

But today, I miss my father.

8

GREEN ELEMENTARY SCHOOL

I WOKE UP IN MY TWIN BED—THE. SHEETS SOAKED MOLDED TO both my skinny body and the thin-sunken mattress. Sweat outlining my body like the broad chalk outline of a homicide on a dirty city street. It takes practice to gain perfection in laying impeccably still during the long hours of a humid summer night. Arms and legs parted away from my body to avoid the ugly feeling of sticking to one's self. Think of it as a snow angel frozen in the act of the broad stroke except it's a corpse stopped in time through the stale night air of summer.

What should be the welcoming warmth of spring turns out instead a miserable early summer in D.C.

This means humidity made unbearable by life without air conditioning. Occasionally, dust swirls trapping trash in an updraft of dry air served as the sole suggestion that a breeze might exist. It's not really a slight wind but more of a rude reminder of what not to expect and what you really get in the projects during summers in the District of Columbia. Even the slightest breeze is hard and bad ass.

I hate this routine. It's time to get out of bed which in one depressed way is welcomed. Sleeping precariously on the edge of the mattress is truly the only semblance of support in the entire bed. I don't remember metal springs jutting through worn material so much as the ache from slipping into the concave shape of a mattress with only one memory—old and used. Ironically, it was the appropriate description of a sinking sensation for my restless young life.

Maybe I brushed teeth and washed my face. It's all a blur. I wasn't really awake. You never go into a deep sleep while positioned to sweat. Ironically, baths occurred at night before a night of steamy induced sweating. I loathed that tub. It didn't matter how fast you were—dirt floated back on you from that which was just cleaned. I was constantly creating waves in the water in an endless battle to ward off returning waves of dirt. The cycle of washing, rinsing, and making waves never ended. I believe even the soap was imbedded with its own dirt. At some point, you simply got out of the tub and wiped the dirt off but only after floating about for the acceptable time measured in the cosmos of Mom's perception of time.

Clothes came from the closet, a pile stashed on the floor of the closet, or crammed in a dresser draw. Socks—once white and now dingy ghetto (I think that's a color)—are the sole selection for every day. According to Mom, a reeking odor created an invisible line barring her from entering the room of me and my older brother. Nonetheless, the stench of old socks and dying shoes didn't prevent her brash words of revulsion from leaping through our doorway. We stank . . . well, off to elementary school!

I didn't know at the time that Green Elementary School was any different from other schools. Yellow buses abound depositing black kids in front of the school from other neighborhoods or project streets. Everyone from 15th Place and surrounding row houses walked their way to school. The route was straightforward and resembled more like a daily migration that turned into repopulation of a small town. Sojourns to school were fun and didn't present the conflict and anxiety born with graduation to junior high school.

My short walk carried me across busy Alabama Avenue in southeast D.C., paralleling the Camp Simms National Guard Depot on one side and low-income apartments on another. Curse words were sometimes shouted out of those apartment windows with meager taunting's of muggings or threats of beatings from some guarding stoops leading into the buildings. Kids in those apartments were more like sophomoric bullies waiting to be called up to the frontlines to become senior project bullies.

Gladly, none of those insinuations materialized, providing a temporary sense of cautious safety and optimism.

THERE WAS A TIME WHEN ADULTS RULED ON 15TH PLACE, AND IT was at Green Elementary. An entirely different environment existed where teachers ruled with the act of pure fear and then some. They had weapons to back them up too and they wielded them with unspoken impunity. Mrs. Donavan was tall and black with a strong voice. She mimicked moms from the projects so there was no kidding or taking directions casually when her voice echoed commands. Mrs. Donavan's classroom was in the main school building. Mr. McNeil, the math teacher, was this enormous structure of a black man who was shaped like a small Sherman tank stood on its end. His nose was wide and big, and he sported an Afro several inches tall that never moved or showed a hair out of place. His appearance reminded me later of an oversized line from the "Mod Squad" show of the early 70s. Mr. McNeil spoke with force and finality. Asking for repeated directions was akin to inviting God himself to rain down with anger and fire. Bullies in training didn't practice their art in his class or on his playground.

I assumed that all teachers carried a kind of sidearm like my teachers. I question whether paddles were sanctioned tools of education, but they were immediately effective if wielded. It didn't matter given paddles were mom approved, mom utilized and encouraged by every adult in the projects.

The paddle carried by Mr. McNeil had the look of a historic artifact used by Moses to whip the Israelites into obedience. The making of Big Bertha had to be measured by cubit feet and fortified by fires from Hell as good measure. Quite striking to any school kid. Mr. McNeil's math class was in the annex across a blacktop, which was a short walk from the back entrances to the school. We practiced addition, multiplication, and subtraction skills for the entire classroom hour every day. I passed every practice with A's but usually failed the real test that followed the practice sessions. There was something about the baritone voice that scared the crap out of me every time he barked the word "begin". It would be easy to forget your own name and birthdate after Mr. McNeil's blaring pronouncements. I wondered if kids were sent to the annex and to Mr. McNeil's room to exact discipline. There was no threat of prying ears alarmed by cries for forgiveness or rescue. Donnie, the worst bully and drug pusher in the school was reduced to crying after a few mighty swings from Big Bertha. Kids talked a lot about everything but mentioning anything about Donnie's spankings were inconceivable. Word would eventually get back to him resulting in something worse than a paddling.

ONE DAY IN AN INSANELY PURE ACT OF SELF-DESTRUCTION, I braved God and took advantage of Mr. McNeil's temporary absence from the classroom. Hunched over, I slivered up to his desk to spy out any information on an upcoming math test. Remember, I was horrible at math. As I leaned over his desk with hands rummaging through papers, the metal door to the classroom swung open. Mr. McNeil stood there with Heaven's gates closing swiftly behind him. I stared in disbelief while the rest of my body was frozen in its convicted stance still bent over the desk. After convincing him that I wasn't the loan criminal, all the boys ended up in the bathroom—lined up for a meeting with Big Bertha. I met that hunk of wood that morning and carried a sting on my rear end that lasted most of the day. I never understood why that effective means of crowd control and education didn't continue into junior high school. It was as if the roles reversed and the kids became the unyielding adults and teachers regressed to frightened followers.

Green Elementary School was one of the few places I looked forward to recess or any break during the school day. We were set free for fifteen to thirty minutes a day to run and play to our hearts delight. I could be found running wildly away—not from bullies, but from heavy-handed Olivia. She chased me all the time shouting "winn-doeew". Her decree was a cry to other girls to join in the chase. Invariably, I ran out of shortcuts and was outnumbered by arms of little girls reaching from everywhere. Once caught, small punches were had until the big-armed and big-fisted Olivia made her way to my arm or chest. I think she liked me a lot because her punches and yells of "winn-doeew" made her smile.

Olivia's smiles really hurt too.

9

THE ROACH HUNTER

MY WEAPONS WERE SKILLED OVER THE YEARS, NOT FROM PROVING grounds spread out and measured in kilometers or acres but earned and marked by feet and inches. This was good ground, fertile, and easily traversed. Squeaky floorboards were well known. Therefore, each step was well-practiced and directed as a chess player whose every move intentional toward the ultimate prize. Like most hunters, patience became the unspoken creed. I was ready with my weapon(s), and heightened my opportunity for conquest, anxiousness, and defeat.

Hello! I'm known as "the Roach Hunter". My past can never be erased or forgotten.

My weapons were simple yet ruthless. Instruments of certain doom and finality were found in their well-worn purpose. Handles shaped by grips of fear and anger. I had no separation of mind and weapon in my savage, unyielding singular purpose– to stalk and destroy. without regret or hesitation. Simultaneously, I became a zealot and dispassionate executioner of a certain species from at least age five. Roaches were the bane of my childhood existence.

My hunting ground was primarily my bedroom followed by the kitchen and dining area. Rooms were in the row house and later in third floor apartments. Today, I would estimate that our average size apartment or row house was approximately 900 to 1100 square feet. My killing field more like a 10 x 10 bedroom with bed, dresser, and closet.

Surprisingly, the enemy was unchanged in look, patterns and actions despite different locations. The shell of a dwelling betrayed the menacing nature within. One could be haunted by the reincarnation of the same forty-seven species of the domesticated *periplaneta americana* or more commonly known as roaches. They were brown to dark brown to reddish brown and even yellowish brown in color. Some were thin and fast while others thick and fat with greed yet still speedy. Antennas swinging wildly about picked up the feel of things in search of the ultimate treasure, food. I had never tried to learn about roaches. I found myself repelled and disguised during my research in writing this chapter. Roaches were as much a part of my childhood life as bullies and government PB&J sandwiches. Therefore, I was more a duty-bound to share my experience.

Their six legs—bony and serrated— used for unwanted entry tattered along our wooden or linoleum floors, echoing invasion. The sound of thousands was readily reduced to five or ten once the quick shutter of a light illuminated their presence. The kitchen was apparently close to the roach home base because their presence at night was overwhelming. Mom kept a spotless kitchen, and open packages were rubber banded and otherwise secured to the point that we had trouble opening a package when needed. I was hungry all the time but could resist temptations to eat at night. Even if I were able to by-pass mom's ultra-sensitive hearing that guarded anything edible, I was in no mood to confront an atrocious colony of devourers.

I was never able to confirm a scouting party from the entire damn army. Scattering became their well-known pattern. The sound of their defeat was a dull squishy noise signaling my victory. It had a similar sound to stepping on a grape or pea. I never grew accustomed to the oozing noise of guts squirting out with white and green glistening matter. Mercy was exercised but only as a second and final swat with overwhelming force to ensure my misery had ended. Cannibalism usually took care of any remains.

The instruments of their demise became my weapons of choice. Worn tennis shoes were always handy. Church shoes, soles hardened and leather shiny for the Lord, were desirable and required little measure for intensity and inevitability. It seemed to take only one blow before searching for the twin or brother. Bodies lay where they were killed as the hunt usually continued. My battle never made it to the strategic purpose of a war of attrition. Their population never did decrease but instead multiplied as if they were bunnies locked in a box without anything else to do but . . . you know, procreate. I used pencils, brooms, and other weapons that could be jammed into corners, under baseboards and into cracks.

The stealth nature of roaches was betrayed only by the sound of scurrying which was at its peak whenever nightfall slipped in or when lights dimmed in my room. I had no night vision equipment except for 100-watt bulbs. Once caught out on the grounds, my innate training assumed action without thought but with rhythmic speed and agility. I was on the hunt.

You might not fully appreciate my commitment and actions. I was the hunter and they were the prey. Snuffing the lives of several enemies within a few seconds of turning lights on was easy.

The search began hovering low just above the floor entrusting senses to be attuned to sound and invisible schematics. Smelly feet never touched floor boards until absolutely necessary. My voice uncontrollably reached its highest pitch; girly in nature at the feel of the creepy dashing across my feet. I am forever certain that each of those six legs could be felt in their motioned sequence trailing over my skin. Hunters have their Achilles heel and mine was a roach crawling over me. Inexhaustible minutes would pass before there was another and another sound echoing in the chambers of my inner ear alarm system. Afterward, an added round of attacks, casualties and victories would occur. It was the nature of things and the expected outcome of boy—the hunter over the hunted.

Furniture would be shoved about indiscriminately. Smelly tennis shoes—mildewed and curled from exceeding their life span—lay atop dirty refuge in my closet providing great but temporary cover for those soldiers. Another shoe in hand swung like a machete clearing out things for better targeting. Sometimes it became not smashing an enemy in his steps but rather smashing where my experience taught me, he was going to be. Got another sucker! One could barely distinguish the sound of two thunderous strikes of the smack of a shoe to floor because of the quickness of my left hand and left shoe. A lefty has a mean curve ball and a wicked overhead shoe swing too.

Some would survive, taking advantage of the death of a relative by making it to the infamous baseboard cover. Wall molding lay above floors creating cavities for hiding. Pennies, school pencils, and brown things accidentally and intentionally found their way under this cover, survivors for a time. There began my waiting game and the making of a legend. An arm arched high in the air with shoe steady in its grip. Breathing shunted instinctively to shallow and muted cycling and body seized in attack position, became my seasoned tactic. I waited and waited to know my enemy could not resist the urge to once again search out sustenance whether in man-made delicacies or of that of a fallen clone. Their habits were predictable and certain. My perch was a chair or creases of a sunken mattress allowing me to extend out over the floor like a diving board over a swimming pool.

At some point, I would tire and call it a successful hunt. Back to bed covers or in most cases lying atop my sweat stained sheets. Although I was the victor, they also claimed a victory as well. I lay tense with hands and feet decidedly away from walls and bedposts. The fewer yet continued scurrying sounds in their own way represented a residual taunting. I could not always take stock of body count the next morning. Sometimes my victories had disappeared or only a leg or other body part remained. I didn't subscribe to the niceties or honors of battle. There were no neutral periods where soldiers could retrieve the injured and dead. Over time, I came to accept the despicable habit of my brown enemies. They ate—no—*devoured*, their own.

Once I went with a friend to get water from his house in the apartments across the street from our row house. We had been playing outside on a hot summer day, so water was a perfect remedy. I couldn't bring anyone in the house whether mom was or wasn't home, so we went to his mom's place. He opened the cabinet above to retrieve glasses and roaches scurried about irritated by invasion of privacy. I don't know if I was more taken by the bright red lipstick stain on my glass or the idea that I was about to drink from glasses that had housed those creatures. They crossed over from infestations of the night to roaches anytime and anywhere. I held the glass of water and put it near my mouth but never drank from it. I also never went inside his mom's apartment again.

This endless warfare faded once I left for college. I was removed completely as I married and moved out of state. Were these the enemy only of my childhood? On occasion, I encounter a relative of a deceased soldier looking to exercise vengeance or, so it seemed. Actually, another bug was at the wrong place and the wrong time and unknowingly messing with the wrong boy—I mean—*man*. My hunter instincts re-ignited and my disdainful nature revived, responding on impulse. From age five to likely a senile man, the hunter in me will never be erased or forgotten. You must understand that I was, and will always be, a roach hunter.

10

YOUR ZIPPER IS OPEN

ANOTHER NORMAL SIGHT IN THIS BARREN LANDSCAPE WAS THE cruel act of pregnancy. I have a fixed memory of this because it crossed my path more than I can say, growing up on 15th Place. How could a girl—a child—beget another child? Which of the two was truly the baby and why didn't anyone have a father?

Today, I can only imagine that to see a young girl's stomach huge and extended was the obvious result of poor education or unprotected sex. I don't think anyone cared about what should or could be protected. It wasn't unusual to see a girl in junior high or even elementary school waddle about with a stomach rupturing through a small pair of Levi's. These weren't stretch waistband jeans designed with pregnancy in mind. They were the same petite size pants fitting tightly over thighs and even tighter over butts flaunting goodies in hopes of attracting someone. It apparently worked.

I was a skinny bow-legged kid with kinky hair at an age when deodorant wasn't staple, and clothes were exchanged for another set of dirty clothes in the hamper. Mom didn't know. She wasn't aware that I thought there were some very cute girls with big brown eyes smiling at me, saying "here I am." They were always in mating season and I suppose at some instinctive level, so was I. I just didn't know it on a mature conscious level or know how to "do it" or even what "it" was. I was worn down by constant arm-to-arm conflicts with two of three sisters who were mortal adversaries. I had no desire at the time to figure out that girl/guy thing. Still, those girls showed everything. They were after us. I could be included in the "us "category or male category due to biology and design. However, it wasn't lost on me that those ten and twelve-year-old *femme fatales* were after other guys who talked with a loose slang and strutted with a harden walk, signifying they were part of the fabric of our stitched together project.

I was the anomaly who enunciated endings to words and spoke with an accent foreign to alleys and gangs. It wasn't my fault. I just came out that way and no matter the attempts. I couldn't convincingly perform or act out as one of the "us". My true nature unintentionally slipped out. I liked history, science, and social studies. I liked to write, and I was curious about stuff outside the invisible yet arresting walls of the project. I was this way in elementary school although it didn't stop me from noticing what everyone else saw. It was almost impossible for a girl to hide the obviousness of pregnancy. I don't think Woolworth's, or the five-and-dime store sold maternity clothes. I didn't know there were such things made specifically for moms-to-be until much later in my prematurely aged life. Girls had only what they had and wore only what they wore. There wasn't much in between.

～

I REMEMBER MANY TIMES SEEING PANTS UNBUTTONED AND WHAT

appeared to be zippers ripped from their notches when a girl four- or six-months pregnant passed by. It may be incredible to accept but I have specific memories about life's cruel joke from the fourth or fifth grade. It's embarrassing to admit naïve thoughts seeing a soon-to-be mother as I walked glass- and weed-littered sidewalks in the neighborhood. My mother would be proud of the polite and discreet way I was thinking of letting this girl know her pants had unknowingly became unsnapped and unzipped. Yep, I was just a nerd no matter how sweet or dear.

As we drew closer, I was overcome with a strong sense that my good intentioned gesture was somehow wrong. I saw the hard, damaged look on her face and figured she was probably twelve or thirteen years old. Her psychotic hairdo unkempt but hand-cuffed in the back by a rubber band and her hardened non-feminine pace was a warning. Instinct—probably self-preservation—shouted inside me to just keep walking. I obeyed, holding my breath under the cover of a deadpan expression. I'm cool. I know what's going on. The I-don't-care-about-you look was the look I hoped to portray. I didn't want the real nerdy and stupid person reeking of fear and disgust from not knowing this preg-nant person was well-aware of her condition and design sense. Maybe she was also portraying a false confidence while knowing deep inside that her life would forever be changed and be confined to the projects of 15th Place. Remember, this place was different. It was more like a huge ice barge at the distant Arctic. It looked starkly bland and unassuming from a distance, but a closer view confirmed huge fractures in its structure and community.

Now she belonged to an unwanted and damaging impression most people outside the projects had of black people. This child strutting down the street also greatly increased her chance of being a permanent residence of the projects and thus a forgotten citizen. It was a model played out that guaranteed what seemed like a perpetuated income constructed by a city run welfare system. I learned never to say anything, to look away in disinterest and just wondered what life might be like for those fine cute little girls.

I saw many girls whose zippers were broken.

11

I WAS NO TYRANNOSAURUS REX. I WAS A PLANT EATER

ONCE UPON A TIME IN A FORGOTTEN LAND, THERE EXISTED LARGE flesh-and-leaf-eating creatures that roamed and ruled vast expanses. An order of dominance played out in every history book. In trying to explain my life in the projects, I find that looking at it as if I had lived in the land of dinosaurs best paints my canvas for others to understand.

I remember reading stories that began with "once upon a time". It was an innocuous and innocent beginning whose end couldn't be determined by title alone. Children's books serve to set the stage for eager imaginations and colorful characters. I was always intrigued with history before realizing certain humans became the dominant species. The difference in a child's fantasy compared to an adult's reality is more about possibilities and seizing opportunities. Something is always possible or at least in adulthood there are realistic hopes and dreams. It ensures a happy ending that we all seek by keeping us just between the magical and reality.

I didn't have a Never Land of pirates and magical dust and fantasies. Instead, my existence seemed more like a world of

Neanderthals—more basic and guttural. In many ways it was simple and basic. I wasn't like those who showed no interest or shame as they extracted bites of meat from my hind. This jungle nature was never bread into my chromosomes. I must have had a missing DNA strand or the hardened trait which was a natural characteristic for anyone in the projects but had skipped a generation with me. Nevertheless, I was caged within this project with man-eaters and all. This was a jungle with carnivores hunting anything that moved. I didn't pace back and forth in a worn path whose boundaries were well-defined and maybe self-imposed as was the case if you lived in public housing. Ironically, I never saw my adversaries beyond the places they roamed—stores, schools, alleyways, or stoops. I'm not sure where they went and what they did once hunger, thirst, quotas for lunch or money were met. Maybe that helped to explain the bottles of Colt 45 and Boon's Farm found everywhere in my land. I could find spent needles and cigarette butts tossed about like resulting trash from a family gathering. It wasn't hidden in a back alley but around the corner from my door and on the way to school.

Occasionally I had the opportunity to see a few specialized creatures from a distance. One group honed the skill of retrieving money while another group was best at beating up others. A stegosaurus with its spiky tail and armored plates was a great defensive tool and its low profile made it easy to consume low-lying bushes and shrubs. I had no defensive or offensive protective plating. I might have seen my nemesis down school hallways or blocks away. This early warning gave me a chance to find another path to class or a wildly circuitous route to get a carton of milk or cigarettes for my mother. It took a lot of circling about to make it before the school bell rang.

I didn't need an anthropologist to describe the carnivore of carnivores. I just needed someone to know that I was more of a plant eater—docile and content to reach for the sweet leaves branched high in the canopies. Most classes in school created an environment for a higher calling. They tasted good and the only thing that could be digested that gave me some hope for something better. I was enabled to discover my intellect—a destiny unknown but possible and a way to sit high above the nature of an otherwise dark and deadly place. It would be easy to conclude that I'm being way too animated and overly dramatic in my descriptions. I would agree if I hadn't experienced it for myself.

My mother said my proper speech and studious look was the most evident sign and invitation for harassment. I was shy. A soft-spoken voice made me stand out. It didn't matter that I was lanky, skinny-as-a-stick and sported an afro that unkempt and uncut. I looked like everyone else. Instinctively, there was something that told the world at 15th Place that I didn't belong. I was fair game. It also resulted in a unique form of hazing and spitefulness as if I were new to the neighborhood or a new kid at school every single day.

My name, Wendell didn't carry an inventive or creative uniqueness. Drea, Juana, or Rashad might have given me a temporary hand up in the neighborhood. There was no room for a timid kid at that time. My dad shuttled the family off to the Philippines during his military career while I was a baby. We made it back in time for Dad to dump us off and for <om to begin the life of a mother raising five children. It began on welfare.

Mom couldn't do anything about my name or my shy demeanor. I asked but she couldn't recall how she arrived at my name. I wasn't named after a relative or any famous people that inspired her at the time. There was no explanation or defense I could use to justify who I was. I remember times when a mother would burst through doorways into the housing court spurting defensive words about her child. Those intended protective shouts were more profanities littered with sporadic English. I never knew what prompted the tirade or whether the obscenities served its purpose. How do you think I would have been treated had my mother confronted my tormentors or showed up at school complaining about me being bullied? I might as well have just gone to school and preemptively killed myself.

Anyway, Mom had her own demons to fight as she struggled with being abandoned by her husband—my father—and raising five children. I'm proud to say that all of my siblings were from the same father. This distinction was somehow important to me because so many kids at that time had brothers and sisters from different fathers. It shouldn't have mattered since we all were project kids, but it did. I desperately wanted some kind of distinction.

Don't misunderstand. There were men in the projects. I saw them standing around on the side of our court or in crowds of other men. They had animated arguments filled with project expletives about football and basketball games. No one watched baseball. There was always talk about "the Man" as the reason for project plight and lack of decent paying jobs. I was too young to think about or recall where anyone worked. A large part of stupid came with being the nerd. I strained to remember any of them living in apartments and row houses that made up the neighborhood. I know they were there. I never met the fathers of my best friends Gerald and Bruce. I guess it was a given that mothers ruled the projects.

As the awkward geek I should have expected to be selected for abuse, periodic attacks, and group jumpings as the awkward geek. It wasn't called being attacked by a gang during my child-hood. We called it being "jumped" which is still very descriptive of what happened. It was something just shy of being mauled. Sometimes, a jumping was actually the act of being piled up on and punched and kicked. Once the attackers were satisfied, they casually walked away as if it were against etiquette to whale on one beyond an agreed time frame. I would guess a two to five-minute beating would get the point across. I never understood the point. Sometimes my pockets weren't riffled through or words spoken. There was no noise but just the sounds of grunts behind the force of kicks and punches.

A wildebeest doesn't have much of a defense when being attacked by determined gators or pack of hyenas. I did have one physical attribute that keep those mauling at bay. Maybe it was a repressive gene that was activated by the fight or flight phenom-ena. I just know that running like a cheetah gave me certain advantage. I could run as if hell itself was chasing me and most times, I could out distance hell. I was fast and running cross-country in secondary school turned my flight into a competitive advantage. Admittedly, I wonder if it was my dazzling and impressive speed or just the laziness of my pursuers that gave me occasional victories. If I won on one day, then I lost big time on the next occurrence. That's if my pursuers remembered that I was the one who got away. Luckily, there were a few more nerdy wildebeest to go around so it may not have made much of a difference if I wasn't jumped on a given day. I must be honest and say that running occurred because I was scared for my life. I couldn't understand why I was singled out for sometimes-daily beatings going to and from school. Summers were temporary reprieves from the daily journeys through the project gauntlet. Why didn't I muster courage to stand up to the Tyrannosaurus Rex? I was not even a mild kind of dinosaur. It's taken much thought and embarrassment to acknowledge the manly short-coming I needed as a child.

ONCE, AFTER HAVING MOVED FROM THE PROJECTS, I WAS WALKING through an area of raised houses where only the floors remained which defined where a row house once stood. I was approached from the opposite direction by a guy looking hard at me. He had this look in his eyes that soon revealed his intention. A demand for all my money was not a surprise. Are you kidding me? Haven't I had enough of this? My adrenaline rushed through my body and mind. We started fighting. I was hitting back although I'm not sure if I landed a punch. I do know that he never landed a good hit either. I had never been so excited and happy to fight anyone. This was the first time I could fight someone and not a bunch of people. There was no gang. I was working hard at beating this guy but suddenly, out of nowhere came another guy who started in on me too. At that point my excitement turned to fear. Where did this guy come from? Did a call for "jumpers" in the nearby area go out so others would soon be joining them? Where are and when will the others join in? Instinct kicked in and I ran, easily losing them. I wish you could have seen the smile on my face as my long legs out-distanced disinterested thugs. I was near jubilant in discovering that I could and wanted to fight back.

"Dumb ass, why didn't you do that all along?"

I often wondered if my life and ability to fight back might have been somehow different had my dad had been around. This might have been a convenient excuse which gave me permission to blame my dad for my lack of guts and fortitude. I still consider the possibility today.

Meanwhile, there was no way of getting around these guys in my younger life. There were times when sheer numbers outweighed the possibility that all could profit. In hindsight, I assumed it was the best and easiest way for them to make a buck. It was like going up to an ATM but never inserting card or pin number yet having money appear. Losing what dollars and coins I had to them after coming out of the grocery store was accomplished in a sort of good-mannered way. The trite command typically uttered was,

"Give me your money!"

The unspoken but well understood statement written across bored and sullen faces that accompanied it. It read with an ultimatum of "or I'll kick your ass."

The look, or statement, was really unnecessary as everyone who was not the intimidator was familiar with the routine. I often wondered if they became familiar with me after so many pocket invasions or did, I simply fit a profile unbecoming of our unhallowed project ground?

There was Boswell who was my height and usually light-skinned though then tanned in the summer with curly brown hair. He wasn't the classic looking project boy. He was a bad guy and a friend, or so I thought. We lived in the same court just a few doors down from each other. Ironically, there were a lot of guys of different colors though clearly black and project-kept. Once Boswell chased, caught, and held me down while others caught up. The routine played out with me being punched and kicked by a group of guys. I wasn't on my game that day and certainly didn't expect my neighbor in the court to be involved. I became Wendell the long neck caught by Boswell the Tyrannosaurus Rex. Mother Nature was at work again.

I feigned pain, yelling at every blow—the kind of yell I did when Mom would give me a spanking. If she thought I was crying hard, then she would stop. The guys soon tired or became bored. When they walked away, I snapped up and jogged away. One of the guys shouted, "hey look," pointing his accusing finger at me as if I violated some long-standing victim rule of not displaying sincere pain and a lengthy recovery. I kept running, peering back to analyze the collective state of mind of my assailants. It was sensible to continue to extend the gap between assailant's fists and my body. I had a sense they had their fill of beating, especially since it was hot and humid.

THE NEXT DAY AT JUNIOR HIGH, BOSWELL, IN A CASUAL AND friendly way, asked how my mother was doing. I liked him and most of time, Boswell was accepting of me. I remember this vividly as it was so strange and surreal to be held down by the guy who was otherwise an okay guy. How does one give pause to aggressive behavior, to give thought to the pain inflicted or the mother of the one being beaten? Maybe Boswell forgot about the day before or was merely fulfilling his role in the pack that day.

I suppose it is prudent not to remain close to those who could change their minds and begin another beating. I've seen nature play out this same scenario of the attackers. There were those who seemed positioned within arm's reach, studying the facial and body language of the prey and willing to help make the ass kicking a reality. "Brothers" waiting near the waterhole were quick to grab the back of your pants if they thought they had a "runner," and even more quick to check your pockets for change.

The Clint Eastwood movie, *"Gauntlet"* gave definition to that time in my life. One definition refers to a military punishment:

> *"A punishment formerly used in the military in which somebody was forced to run between two lines of men armed with weapons who beat him as he passed."*

That description sounds awfully familiar, but it was more about the row of guys waiting for some kind of payday off the backs of kids like me. I'm not sure any booty was shared but there was a sense of enjoyment, given there was nothing else to do on a hot day in the Serengeti. Wintertime was a welcome relief as those in waiting were often reduced to one or two stalkers. Occasionally, I caught a break when none stood guard. I guess the pocketful of return didn't outweigh the damp, bone chilling cold weather. Interestingly, as I remember those rare, "jump free" days, I was probably more terrified by the possibility that someone was late coming on guard and would rush to catch up on the day. It was easier to accept that which was seen and known than the unknown even if it meant losing your money or taking a few punches.

THERE WAS ONE PLACE WHERE THOSE DAILY HARDENED characters never attempted to cross. History class ruled. Here, I was the dominant beast, although I didn't have any menacing or fearful traits. Maybe it was my very own sanctuary and land of discovery. My brain was able to walk the fields of slavery even though school books sorely lacked a full and complete historical picture. My interest was also peaked as I read about the wars of these United States. I had a chance to think about life in the thirteen colonies and marvel at how a land grew into a nation.

Mr. Jones, my junior high school history teacher, was a rare patriarch in my world. He introduced me to the enormity of learning and the potential of my mind. I loved history and still call it my favorite subject. In some way history allowed my mind to suspend current reality

I passed every history test with 100% and then some whenever there were extra credit questions. Why not? I was good at remembering everything. At one point, Mr. Jones gave up and said there was nothing more he could teach me. At that point, he allowed me to create a few tests for the class. I didn't make them easy either so Mr. Jones balanced them out with a little give-them-a-chance question. This was our secret and was to never to be revealed unless death or dismemberment was imminent. Had my non-jovial classmates ever caught wind of this, my body would not have been discovered for weeks—yet another unsolved murder for the books of the D.C. Given the noise of inner city living, I doubt anyone would have noticed or heard a Wendell being beaten to death over a history test.

How would a leaf eater get away from the veraciousness of Tyrannosaurus Rex? I don't imagine a dinosaur taking the long way around the valley in hopes of making for a less stressful day. I really didn't have alternative routes except a few plans:

Plan A

Proceed straight through the forbidden territory and take a chance that the meat eaters had already tasted their fair share of other Wendells. That was a roll of the dice.

Plan B

I could take this approach which involved skirting the stalking grounds by walking just to the back and outside of their home ground. Again, this roundabout was another chance but held dire consequences if detected.

Plan C

This was the more desired route, but it took time. The course involved taking an extremely circuitous path that appeared to go in the opposite direction but had a planned swing back when least expected.

I CONSIDERED EACH OPTION EVERY MORNING AND AFTERNOON AND waited for the unanticipated Plan D to materialize. It was like opening the refrigerator repeatedly, hoping a new foodstuff would suddenly appear. I could not come up with a new and inventive plan. Every outing to and from junior high school became a roll of the dice.

One might expect that once surviving the daily dreadful waters from home to school, there would be safety and relief in school hallways and classes. That was not the case. Security was not to be found among teachers and school administrators. They, too, swam their own fearful and tenuous course on a daily basis. It was not surprising when a teacher returned to the island with black eyes or other physical display of an encounter. Car tires might have been slashed or windows shattered by a killer orca whale or two. Perpetrators were known, and justifications well practiced. Maybe it was a teacher who called out an orca embarrassing his mean persona by asking him to read a passage displaying the command of an illiterate. Perhaps a teacher even dared to report unacceptable behavior to the principal's office resulting in suspension or other disciplinary action. On those occasions a killer whale might brazenly come ashore to devour and reclaim reputation. The next day he—or occasionally she—would return to school unscathed. The teacher followed a day or two later but scathed and docile. I quickly learned that students and teachers were always considered prey and the sturdy brick walls and mortar of my junior high school was a mere illusion of shelter. There lies the contradiction, teachers not safe in the supposedly safe place.

To my disbelief and ultimate irony, high school became a peninsula to something larger and free from marauding predators. Thank goodness for Frank W. Ballou High School. It was as if I crossed a mountaintop and descended into a land of peace and plenty. My adversaries didn't make that climb because either they weren't interested, or they were sorely unprepared, thus held back from the journey. Actually, I still wonder if they were perfectly comfortable in the projects, content to circle and dominate as a lifetime profession.

12

SOUNDS

SOUNDS HAD AND STILL DO CAUSE A HUGE AND OFTEN ANXIOUS reaction in my life. I've never quite adjusted to quiet which seems held captive deep within a world besieged by the noise of recklessness and regular ambivalence. People perpetrated horrible acts against one another which were always noisy and unbelievable sad. Yet the brash and loudest noise for me was that of malcontent, of anxiety, and of the stress of daily being in my projects of 15th Place. The unease each morning was tampered a bit by the steady rhythm of sounds as I left my row house door and court. The familiar decibel of cars driving by, tires screeching and people talking loudly as if the world was deaf, radiated from windows and corners instinctive to inner city existence. It brought comfort and intrigue for me even as a young elementary school student. This is how life was around the world. Right?

Cars made their presence known not with smooth purring engines but by catalytic converters that had long lost life and holes in mufflers strapped to the undercarriage by wire or non-existing clamps. City buses made rushed stops as if to stay just ahead of some imminent danger. Other sounds such as racing fire trucks, ambulances and the constant barrage of sirens from police cars served as background music, helping to define my urban boundaries.

And there in the midst was this kid who was and continued to expand into something different. A kid with his own special noise. Despite my shyness, there was this hyperactive, tangled, and sometimes loud kid when left to his own inventiveness. That's when I stood out like a jacket made of tweed and checker board squares.

These strangely comforting noises never abated. The constancy over time became expected and familiar. I loved listening to my surroundings as I slept with open windows to cool my back from humid summer nights. They sort of canceled themselves out, like white noise. Those were background or supporting chores for the many voices that filled the air.

Sometimes the voice was Mom, calling out from the front door or bedroom window. She would shout each of our names with a threatening tone that it was dinnertime. Other moms (remember no dad sounds anywhere) were calling so-and-so child to,

"Get your big, black ass to the house!"

"Don't talk back to me!"

"Or I'll kick your ass!"

You could also hear echoes of girls with shrill voices on the front porch trying to catch a breeze. The guys would be on curbsides or leaning on treasured cars having their own "brother" talk. By junior high school, most guy talk centered on hitting some fine booty and sports. Project slang was made more imperceptible due to the buzz of Colt 45 or Boon's Farm or weed smoked brazenly while police cars cruised by. The sounds of thuds and rocks ricocheting off trash cans or bottles crashing were all part of play. There was plenty of laughter as kids found the means to have fun. I did too.

IT WAS THE SHEER ABSENCE OF NOISE THAT BECAME THE MOST frightening for me. Stillness, an air of perfect peace and harmony was a rarity. When it did happen, silence became overwhelmingly loud and mysterious compared to the anger city noise seemed to emit. My familiar sounds, keen to my ears, could easily distinguish passiveness from that which could harm. I didn't need to hear the words "Danger, Will Robinson," from the television show *Lost in Space*. I could feel it in my bones and crawling down my skin. Those sensations guided my very presence in my own project.

Just as I became accustomed to my surroundings, Mom decided my sister and I needed to experience something different. So, off to camp we went for a two-week stint every summer for three years. I suspect the roughly 336 hours of woodsy time was to offer one a break from challenging and hyperactive kids during steamy summers when overactive children could find absolutely nothing to do but boil into arguments. For those consecutive summers we were taken to Southwest Washington at Jefferson Jr. High School to join what appeared to be millions upon millions of other kids. It was probably only hundreds of inner-city kids ranging from ages five to fifteen, but it seemed like every black kid in D.C. was being shipped off at the same time. Imagine D-Day in Prince William Forest Park. We were coming in force and quite a landing it would be.

Well, we were off to what could have easily been Nottingham Forrest in the hills of Triangle, Virginia. It was probably a good thing that the camp was bounded to the south by the Marine Corps Base Quantico as a man-made force to contain what would swell the tiny population in Prince William County, VA. Census data shows Triangle as a total area of a mere 2.6 square miles. I'm certain shades of blackness densely occupied at least 2.5 of those miles for two-week stints throughout the summer.

One was lucky if he had a friend going to the same place at the same time and ended up in the same cabin. I was very lucky in that at least there was one person I knew who would end up saving me a few times as well. That was my cousin Daryl. We grew up together, each in his own project but connected by a half mile of safe ground. I usually walked to his mom's apartment without having to worry about being harassed or chased. Except for Daryl, it seemed everyone else knew everyone else but me. Even Daryl knew camp counselors, cabins, the lake and every tree in the woods. We were in Camp Cherokee, which was one of five camps. My sister was a two-mile hike away at Camp Goodwill.

It really didn't matter that I didn't want to camp. My shyness had no say in the decision during the first summer. I lined up, was checked off, accounted for, and bused to the woods where black kids went for the summer. I would be introduced to weird and scary noises newly discovered for this project kid.

I don't remember the bus ride but very clearly recall Camp Pleasant. Befitting of our rustic surroundings, we were housed in bona fide log cabins. Each cabin held bunk beds housing sixteen kids. In the middle of the cabin just off center of the doorway were a head counselor and an assistant counselor. Counselors were there to guide inner-city kids in the act of having fun in the woods.

Therefore, it would also have been reasonable that black kids would give similar guidance had any white or black counselor came to inner city projects for two weeks. Surely this hardened forest was new and unfamiliar territory to white people and maybe some blacks. The exception was the "Poe-leece" (police) who occasionally drove through the neighborhood but never actually stopped or got out of their patrol cars. I wonder if they locked their doors too while driving by in a mood to protect and serve.

As you might expect, long hikes were had along worn paths that wove through dense brush and trees. I strained my eyes staring at a given spot or a certain location because of leaves rustling or the sounds of little footprints paralleling the long line of inner-city noises which defined our presence. We were loud, stubborn chatterboxes, full of strife and laughter, always in a state of making fun of each other. The fun was littered with exchanges of "Motherfucker" that and "shit" this and "I ain't doin' that," and "I ain't listening to no white man either".

You could count on hearing something like "he ain't my daddy," as justification for everything.

Those statements mired in attitude were dead on. I'm not sure anyone knew his father. I sure didn't know my daddy at the time. Being obstinate and refusing to listen to the "white man" would have been more consistent with the culture and environment; therefore, resistance and rebellion were usual outcomes.

I had no choice words of ugliness to speak. I tried it a few times behind closed doors but couldn't muster the guts to say stuff like that in public. If my mom ever found out, she would have beaten the shit out of me.

I was comfortable with that word under my breath but felt it more accepting to "damn" whenever possible. Admittedly, that didn't occur often. However, any attempt had to be accomplished in a cool relaxed way as if it were a regular part of my everyday bad self. Those damned Puffed Wheat or crazy ass Rice Krispie cereal. A three or four-word vocabulary of profanities really didn't help in my effort to blend in. The lack of 15th Street dialect and ever-present proper language served as another immediate sign that I didn't fit in.

I heard "You're just trying to be white" many times during junior high school years. In fact, I was just being and doing what came naturally and wasn't trying to do anything more. I just wasn't certain how to be blacker than what I was born to be.

AN ENTIRELY NEW SPECTRUM OF SOUNDS AND EXPERIENCES WERE introduced to me at Camp Pleasant. I give significant credit to my cousin Daryl who has a rock-solid memory of the details of our time at camp. I attended camp over a three-year period from ages ten through twelve. Daryl and I went to camp a few of those years together. We were never in the same cabin, but he was my "big brother" of sorts, protecting me from the bullies transplanted from inner city D.C. along with the rest of us.

I have many gaps in my early life where memories seemed to have been taken in the middle of the night never to be recalled again. Daryl helped me to fill in the missing pieces about Camp Pleasant. I've pondered whether dramatic events ripped those memories out of my mind.

Walking the trails meandering through Camp Pleasant was a daily activity. You can take the kid out of the projects, but you couldn't take the projects out of the kid. This was apparent following those trails. The wild stompings of little feet were overshadowed by project language sloshing and spilling about like overfilled water jugs.

SOMETIMES I BECAME QUIET AS WE TRAILED ONE ANOTHER, suspicious at what lay behind fallen trees and the camouflage of dense underbrush. I was certain someone or something had selected me out of hundreds to stalk and to hunt. Its true nature would be revealed if only I could stare at one spot long enough. However, I must continue with the newly formed summer camp tribe. Plus, it was difficult to walk, and stare given all the booby traps planted throughout the trails. Vines positioned as snares, branches arched back as catapults for each kid to launch them in the face of the next trailing walker. There were perfect rocks to launch at trees despite warnings from counselors about what not to do. Hey, we knew about throwing rocks. These were just like project rocks that broke windows and bottles or dented siding and trash cans. The resulting sound of projectiles tearing through canopies and suddenly kidnapped into silence was something new. All said, we were a noisy intrusion into tranquility itself.

Mother Nature returned the invasive favor when nightfall came. She introduced a torrent of wilderness sounds not meant for the delicate ears of city boys. Leaves rustled just out of sight as if some creature was dining on the biggest celery sticks ever grown. Thuds, crunches, and animalistic wailings were broadcast throughout the night. There were other sounds that didn't match the short popping burst of gunfire or screams echoing across the row houses back home. Instead, I heard screeching hellish yells coursing through the forest aimed directly at my wooden window. Where did they get those owls from anyway?

Someone kept propping my window open every night, which was strictly against my wishes. Crickets and a cacophony of noises from every species of frogs filled in whenever there was a possibility of quietness. It didn't matter how many times courage was summoned to peer out the cabin window just below my bunk, I could never find the culprits. Then there were the heavy poundings of coconuts dropping from heaven itself. I searched many times in the morning for them but apparently counselors collected the coconuts before kids awoke. How could they expect any kid to sleep with this racket running uncontrollably in all sorts of directions every night? It was deafening and nerve racking. I was exhausted every morning as I protected myself and likely saved every project kid from the beastly unknowns.

Thank goodness for Ms. Bee according to Daryl. I wish I could remember this shy kid's savior. She was a big black lady who ran the kitchen and somehow reminded every kid of grandma back home. You could disrespect a counselor and show distain for others, but no kid dared to disobey anyone who looked like grandma. Every day at lunch and dinner time, all the kids came together to honor in song our temporary grandma. Some jumped atop tables and the rhythm of song began.

"Ms. Bee, you cook so good for me. Hey! Hey!"

The verse repeated itself, I guess until we got hungry. Not much on lyrics but the point was well made. This was the one time where I fit in and belonged. I never recall having this same sense of acceptance until mid-way through high school.

Nighttime at Camp Pleasant did introduce my favorite activity. There was something so special about campfires. Don't get me wrong. I have seen fires on many occasions. There's nothing like seeing a car ablaze or a dumpster set afire or an occasional grease fire consume an apartment. The smell of rubber, plastic, and furniture burnt to shards was always alluring and exciting. However, I never really heard a fire that didn't involve fire fighters breaking windows or punching through walls and ceilings.

Campfires carried different music. It sounded out unusual beats and percussions. Sometimes the sound of crackling wood was overtaken by combustion bursting with flames and heat. Every fiery hot ember had a unique low pitch orchestrated into quietness of the night air. The huge crackling weight of the tall tent of burning wood falling in on itself was mesmerizing. Sparks and embers filled the darkness like fireflies scampering off in a rush. I didn't have to worry about looking over my shoulder or hear the constant barrage of city noise and wonder who did what. It was nice to relax and hear nothing and become lost in the flames. I think it was one of those nights that I learned to sing, "Come by Here, Lord."

Those calming nights were replaced during the daytime by reminders of home. Again, my cousin Daryl shared the story of one particular bully who picked on me and other kids. Once Daryl, warned him to leave his "cuz" alone. What a mistake this kid made when he swung at my huge, solid and big fisted "cuz." Daryl wasn't a hardcore project kid, but you didn't mess with him either. After a last warning in the form of a push, that kid's wild punch missed but Daryl's didn't. Surprisingly, that kid lived and unfortunately, both got in big trouble. I didn't have any other problems at camp that summer. I think every nerd needs a Daryl in his or her life.

I FOLLOWED SUIT IN A WAY BY TAKING ON A PROTECTIVE ROLE FOR my baby sister who is two years younger. A few times we were led on a hike to the girl's camp. We weren't allowed any kind of fraternizing other than daytime visits. Once during a visit, a kid was harassing and chasing after Marjorie. It was obvious that my sister didn't like the taunting. I didn't take well to the kid liking my sister. Daryl and I were walking near a pond that served as the girl's swimming pool. Coincidently, that kid was near the water's edge. Daryl was aiming to push him in the pond, but I beat him to it. A thrashing splash followed, and Daryl and I ran off.

Go figure! Freaking Wendell defending his sister. I must have been overcome by a momentary "instinctiveness" to protect despite not really liking my sister at the time.

There were other sounds, which were very much like home and they were a routine occurrence. It had more to do with being overly energetic coupled with fearlessness. Visiting the camps infirmary or nearby hospital became a routine occurrence every summer.

I like to think I was still learning to use my lanky and flexible body, so accidents were bound to occur. I was hauled off and rushed to the emergency room of the closest hospital every year at Camp Pleasant.

It wasn't my fault that some kid kicked a nest of bees along our trail. Three or four campers were treated in the ER. I received several stings in the head and at least one kid was stung dozens of times. I wasn't to blame either for my last camp related visit to the ER. Campers from several cabins were returning to camp at night following a dim beam of only one flashlight held by a counselor. Like horses spontaneously erupting into a gallop at the sight of barn and hay, we started into a mad dash in the dark at the sight of our cabins in the distance. As tired as we were, the sight of the cabins created its own excitement.

Once again there were familiar emergency room lights and sounds of doctors examining my wounds. During the rush, I tripped and fell face first into the jagged remains of a small broken sapling. My screaming easily matched the screeching sounds of owls in the quiet of the night. I remember the counselor scooping me up and running to cabin, then the car and racing to the hospital. The stab-and-slicing action of the tree cut an arch around the bottom of my eye, just missing my eyeball. According to Mom, the emergency room became a favorite place growing up. She said nurses and doctors were fairly used to seeing me. I was serious at playing in the woods at camp or streets of the projects.

13

THE TASTE OF BEING AFRAID

"A boy's life is not all comedy; much of the tragic enters into it."

— From "Neither", an autobiography (1959)

I think we all have experienced anxiety over passing a test or engaging in something that challenged ability or intelligence. There's the dread of having to confess to breaking a prized possession or being caught in a lie or having your hand "in the cookie jar" of sorts. If I were a cat, my back would arch high and hairs would stand on end in anticipation of attack.

But fear is something deeper, uneasy, and guttural inside. It's an innate early warning system. Fear tells you something is in the air and it's palpable or it might signal something is awfully wrong. In response, mental alarms stiffen muscles to the ready and eyes become acutely aware of surroundings. My fear, induced by project living, was real, protective and even came with a clinical diagnosis.

As I think back about the genesis of well-practiced reactions to my environment, something disturbing was evoked, a strange feeling which had festered like an infection just below the surface of a wound. There lay my innocence—damaged. Below the skin at the under belly, a greater cruelty deepened my contamination.

I carried a distinct, recognizable reflection of a panicked and threatened life. I was always scared. There were times when I simply grew tired of being afraid, but I didn't know how to shut it off. It was a shuddering, a heaving beneath my concave chest, radiating down my bow-legged and bony structure and out of my stick-like arms. This is an occasion where my memory forcibly breaks through and is shoved out of its self-imposed vow of emotional and psychological banishment. For me, fear was propelled by some invisible anger, agitated and confrontational. Being black was its own bound tension. It was tightly stretched skin of a snare drum—ready for play. That tautness couldn't be unraveled in a glass-strewn back alley, under the dim lights of the back stoop, or in the mold-filled corners of a bathroom situated in what was supposed to be home.

I resented this instrument consigned to me. Why did I have to be afraid? Why were others so intent on creating this animalistic world where I was invariably the weak and hunted? It was music that I didn't know how to play. As this life sat before me, it seemed to have a cold, dampening effect on my spirit for more years than seemed proportionally fair. To this day, it still haunts me.

MY INNER TREMOR CAME FROM STEPPING INTO A WORLD FAMILIAR, yet unwanted, into a place that didn't much care for me. Its mantra and unashamed nature easily reflected:

"You have no meaning or value."

My environment hung heavy and dangerous. If I stepped outside of my fortress, our row house, then it was time to be afraid. Imminent and growing danger was constantly signalled as I walked from one block to another toward school. Who will beat on me today? Did I do something to deserve a jumping? Maybe I was simply not black enough on a given day. My mind raced, and my head swivelled wherever I walked. My radar became prudent but telling as it somehow informed others of my presence.

That coolness could be translated into a physical manifestation: a cold shiver, heightened senses, and even goose bumps. A chameleon easily blends in when it learns to resemble surroundings. Although insignificant and somewhat diminutive, I stood out—my black color never providing enough camouflage to safeguard me. I was no chameleon; I was both obvious and discarded. I'm not sure it makes sense, but in a way, I can visualize the taste and texture of my tumult, of my trepidation as it grew into fright and eventually panic on a daily basis. It was rough and coarse, filthy with embarrassment and self-loathing.

My constant agonizing created a desperation all its own, seeking escape and solitude. I believed deeply to the roots of my nappy afro that I didn't belong. It seemed that if I carried books, then I didn't belong. Eagerly raising a hand to answer a teacher's question put me at risk of arousing the ire of someone. Even my hair speckled with lint and dandruff, snared by tangles that no comb or pick could penetrate, didn't waive distain or otherwise grant me membership to the other side of the sidewalk. I just knew to be afraid.

I shared with my primary physician concerns about recurrent behavior and symptoms rather unbecoming of a mid-level executive. I was jumpy and reacted uncontrollably when approached from behind. My sudden and overly animated physical jerks, jumps or defensive posture overtook rational behavior without thought or pause. It was more like a convulsive seizure with arms wailing about as my body jerked around defensively. My voice, swift to crack with indescribable sounds, helped to ready me for attack. My jitters became so bad and constant in adulthood that I would react wildly to co-workers entering my space unexpectedly. It wouldn't be unusual for me to shout and toss whatever was in my hands; papers, pens, or coffee spewed in all directions. It didn't matter if it was friend, peer, or boss. In turn, my action would cause a cascading reaction from the once calm and innocent person who acted as the trigger.

My physician probed further and learned about my childhood. Surviving in the projects was one of continuously being aware of surroundings, what or who to avoid, and what to expect when you least expected anything. The doctor rather casually, and in a matter of fact tone, suggested that I was suffering from Post-Traumatic Stress Disorder (PTSD). I had all of the classic symptoms of a soldier exposed to constant danger and the adrenaline rush that never turned off. PTSD is defined as:

> *"A lasting consequence of traumatic ordeals that cause intense fear, helplessness, or horror, such as a sexual or physical assault, the unexpected death of a loved one, an accident, war, or natural disaster"*

Medical literature explains the symptoms of PTSD as "a severe trauma or a life-threatening event which could have associated signs including depression, anxiousness, vivid memories or flashbacks."

Finally! It all made sense. I have never served in the armed forces or been subjected to a major catastrophic life-changing event. Nonetheless, my jittery reactions to the unanticipated were founded in a war, in my very own personal conflict. One can only imagine that the exposure to the horrifying realities of battle, death and the struggle for one's very life as a soldier are intense and unfathomable compared to anything I've experienced. Yet, I found a reasonable explanation that my brain could wrap around and accept.

This was freeing for me at least for a brief time. The explanation and research itself calmed my skittishness. Unfortunately, the knowledge didn't completely erase a life of practiced responses. The intensity of my childhood trauma had been seared in my mental synapses. Adrenaline-fired defense mechanisms remain at high alert although childhood has long since passed. I learned to be afraid for self- preservation.

Regrettably, my automatic and quick response to the unexpected voice over my shoulder or the presence of someone just out of view did return. I'm more likely to react out of control when expelling my surroundings in order to focus on an important assignment, task or work. Nonetheless, I'm a little more relaxed knowing I can internalize and say,

"Hello, my name is Wendell P. and I was afraid".

14

GAPS

"Hey! Wendell! Is that you?"

THAT WAS THE MALE VOICE ECHOING ACROSS THE LANES AT A convenience store gas pump some fifteen years ago as I was visiting home in southeast D. C. The gas station was just down the street from Sears on Stanton Road. I hesitantly replied "hey"—not really knowing whom it was that was smiling at me expectantly. In actuality, all I could think was,

"Who is this stranger? How did he know my name?"

Apparently, my quizzical expression cued the voice into providing background information to jar my memory. He said "It's me. We used to play at each other's houses every day." My expression remained unchanged reflecting uncertainty. My cousin was with me at the time and repeated the same words, as if it was poor hearing that interfered with a soulful reunion with this stranger.

"You guys were best friends."

I had a complete memory lapse and continue to have a void. The boyhood friend and even my cousin were surprised by my total lack of recall. I finished pumping and paying for gas and expressed my appreciation for him recognizing me. I was being polite, although nothing about the voice, the man, or the background details of childhood play rang true to me.

That is only one of many memory gaps associated with living in the projects on 15th Place. My sister claims that she too, suffers from the same unnamed malady and though unclear, she's certain something happened in our lives to mar our memories. Absentmindedness simply doesn't justify these black holes.

I spent most of my project time growing up with my cousin, Daryl. We played and ran and dreamt together. I remember quite a bit about those times. Undeniably, there are entire segments where there is not only the lack of memory but also a complete gap in time. I struggle to accept an alternative logic involving physical and emotional issues introduced in my tender young life. How does one forget playtime at the home of a best friend while remembering vividly other details? Could I be suffering from permanent mental gulfs? I'm aware of one experience and its influence and have pieces of others for which a manic and damaging influence was the likely outcome.

What I witnessed involved a physically traumatic event, which occurred around age ten or eleven. My memory goes on as if I'm reading an interesting story but at the turn of the page, script is missing, erased, or torn out by a thief in the night. Those pages have never returned or been recreated except for bits and parts pieced together by my mother or siblings.

∾

I DELIGHTFULLY REMEMBER PLAYING FOOTBALL IN A SIDE LOT OF A single-family house not too far from our project court. It was an old house readily found on a rural road but dropped out of place just down the street from our project borders. One side of this play area bordered the National Guard depot—Camp Simms. I used to look through the tall fences mounted with barbed wire at the official military trucks, gas tankers, and other vehicles. On a rare occasion, I managed to see convoys trailing in or out of this base across the street from my project. I never knew where the trail of vehicles went or what they did when they got there. Sometimes, I thought they just went for an official weekend ride.

One side of Camp Simms also served as a high wall for a large open pit. It would remind you of a block-sized area depleted of all its mineral resources, leaving a huge hole. I'm not certain what was previously there, but weather and erosion made for a perfect hill to run up and down during hot summer days—leaving wakes of dust and dirt. It also was a perfect hill for winter sledding with cardboard boxes, trashcan lids or whatever else one could find to sit on. I remember loving to play there because no imminent threats lingered about. It was an unspoken "play safe" area somehow off limits to the bullies in the projects. I assumed they had long lost the art and desire for playtime. It was kid stuff, unworthy of their time.

This strip of open grassy area situated atop the dirt canyon was perfectly designed for tackle football. I was the wide receiver, out-running most any kid. My long skinny legs would propel me like an antelope catching stride, surpassing others. In one perfect long pass, I was in full stride looking into the sky, arms extended and hands steady and ready for the overhead catch. This was one of my budding specialties in our non-super bowl playoff of the year which occurred weekly if not daily. I would instinctively sacrifice and suffer whatever pain and injury necessary for that pro like fingertip catch.

In this particular case, that's exactly what I did. Unfortunately, I didn't notice in my full out stride, the thick telephone like wire stretched from a swing set at one end and grooved into a tree trunk at the other end. I think this was someone's version of a clothesline. Ironically, I remember running into this wire and being close lined from my right ear and half my neck. My next memory was that of waking up to emergency room doctors asking me my name, where I lived, and who I was. I can laugh today as it makes me think about the movie *ET* as scientists and doctors swarm over the lovable alien being.

My mother confirms my spotty recollection. She tells me how on one hot summer afternoon, there was a knock at the back door of our house in the court. She opened it, to find me standing dazed and showing what appeared to be a huge rope burn across my neck. She heard sounds of kids running away with the fleeing words, "We didn't do nothing!"

At least they got me home. I still don't recall the event to this day other than reaching out for the football—another touchdown in the making. I wonder if I caught the football. Over the following week, Mom was able to recreate exactly what happened. I didn't and still don't remember the names of the kids playing football on that fateful day. Neither do I recall walking home, being walked, dragged, carried or otherwise guided and positioned on the back-door stoop. I was kept overnight at the hospital for observation and released the next day. There were no significant injuries although I went home with a huge stark white bandage pasted against my glistening black skin as if surgically positioned from my right ear across my neck in order to keep my head attached to my body.

It was from here on that I find gaps in memory, a twilight where I was certain something had to have happened in some outer limits, but I had no ability to retrieve it. Perhaps my sister and I as kids willingly succumbed to our personal, merciful aura of forgetfulness. Certain events remain vividly burned into thoughts while the full details and other circumstances remain ragged or completely shredded and obliterated.

I had two such emotional moments as a child associated with my father. Dad abandoned his wife, mother, and children when I was three or four years old and well before I started elementary school. Consequently, an unemployed mother was cast in a play she had not studied for. Our family had no choice but to rely on public assistance (we called it welfare) for support.

The first of only two memories as a child of dad occurred in the Philippines. Dad was in supply and logistics in the Air Force.

One day as I sat in the passenger seat while Dad drove, we came upon a major car accident. My dad pulled over, retrieved his first aid kit, and left me in the car while he helped the injured. Dad confirmed my recollection of the event and the twin bridges we were on. My mother also confirmed my memory of living in a house surrounded by thatch roof huts on tall stilts. The house was always overrun with lizards. Mom says I was probably about three years old.

The only other memory I have of Dad was certainly full of emotion, passion, and horror for me. I was at the center of it all. We lived in a row house after returning from the Philippines. Mom had a strong memory of that nighttime event and shared it with me several years ago. My memory is ignited by an argument between Mom and Dad. It occurred outside my parent's bedroom. I was somehow at the center of this epic exchange. Dad was pulling me by one arm and Mom stretching skin and bones of my other arm. They were screaming at each other. I was horrified as Mom's facial muscles flexed in rage, eyes bulged manically, and words pierced me in route to Dad's presence. In this melee my father managed to yank me free of my mother's grip. I was thrown like a rag doll into the master bedroom, barely secured from the pounding from mom's fists.

The argument and yelling continued with only the bedroom door acting as a silent yet immovable moderator separating pure hatred but not the antagonism and intimidation of their voices. Then suddenly, a loud crash followed by the fading voice of Mom as she made her way down the stairs. After a few moments, Dad held me back as if protecting me from a hungry lioness primed just out of sight. He cautiously opened the door. There broken and splintered on the floor was a wooden model ship. It used to sit atop a stand just outside the bedroom door. Mom had thrown it out of frustration, knowing she could never pry the door open against the strong body of the lion—my dad. She didn't remember the reason for the argument or why I was in the middle of it. I do strongly recall the sheer terror of that night like a foul stink forcing its way into my memory.

One of my sisters was aware of another harsh and abusive exchange between Mom and Dad. She only hinted at them, as if honoring my gentle spirit and helping to maintain the black hole, which has kept me safe from the blunt realities of that time. Dad left the family and didn't reappear in my life until my sophomore year in college.

Why would those memories stick in my thoughts like flypaper

trapping a nuisance? Could that afternoon, reaching for my touch down, have given me a blessing in disguise, the gift of forgetfulness? I'm not one to explore these gaps further through hypnosis or psychotherapy. I'm not ready to discover the truth even today. Maybe there will be a time around the age of eighty when I will not remember what was remembered anyway.

15

TO INFINITY AND BEYOND

"Buzz, you could have defeated Zurg all along! You've just got to believe in yourself."

— TOY STORY (1995)

I SUSPECT REMINISCING ABOUT THE MOVIE *TOY STORY* AND quoting a character from the Disney movie is a most unusual way to relate my experience and influences in my little southeast project in the District of Columbia. It undeniably defines the tenor of my success today. My early life was a Pixar production or a laughable cartoon by any means.

Buzz Lightyear eventually discovers his true toy existence. He also finds the courage to accept his nature. Bound with others, Buzz is able to exceed his station in toy land and with help, ultimately finds himself.

Therefore, it is energetic of me to relate my success today to a movie meant for children. Yet, it is within this childhood that I began to find my infinity and possibilities, with the help of a few inspiring school teachers and the challenge of extraordinary summer jobs. In *Toy Story,* the center of attention is Woody, but a host of other characters gave body and context to the movie. It's a stretch, but I could be a Woody with a host of best supporting actors.

My math teacher, Mr. McNeil, who was husky, thick and over-bearing, was my first black male teacher. He mainly struck fear in my little frame, so much so, that every resonating blast of his ominous voice, signaling the beginning and end of a timed math quiz, was a frightening shock to my senses. How did this big black man contribute to my success? Mr. McNeil was relentless in ruling over me and others in this elementary school of all black kids. He forced studiousness, discipline and application even if it was out of pure fear. I also credit him for being the first black male role model where rare stars orbiting the skies of my neighborhood.

My response to Mr. McNeil mirrored the same reaction when realizing a group of guys were about to jump or beat me up. First, temporary paralysis, then senses would recover, and the reality of the moment would kick my mind into frenzy. Practice sessions seemed less threatening, so every practice was passed with straight A's. Unfortunately, that didn't carry over to the actual quiz. I earned an F on every single math quiz. Thank goodness there was homework and other less vocally terrifying math work.

In a way, math became a trial which I failed miserably in high school and succeeded in remarkably at the same time. It, too, was a personal and positive influence as I matured.

I still carry anxiety borne from the foghorn-like shouts from Mr. McNeil. Despite my fear of math, it did teach me a certain grounding and determination. By the time I was mid-way through Frank W. Ballou High School, I was struggling with

Algebra. It was and still is all backwards in my mind. I earned two more years of C's while unable to master those mixed up equations. There went my record for earning nearly all A's. Why did I need to convert or flip a fraction over in order to somehow make it right? Why don't they do it the correct way from the beginning? I never won that debate.

Then there was Geometry, a class that was well ahead of my ability to consume and spit out answers in rapid fire. I earned a whopping big fat F that semester. That was appalling to this kid, who by now was practically an A student. I took a different tact by enrolling in Geometry again but under a different teacher, Mrs. Norwood. Isosceles triangles, rhombuses, trapezoids. and others all came to life. It finally made sense and my mind could grasp it in a sideways sort of way. I received an A in Geometry that year and became Vice President of the Math Club as well as winning honorable mention in the Math and Science fair in Washington, D.C. Admittedly, I continued to struggle with math throughout college. Nonetheless, I learned to grit my teeth and give an A-effort in order to earn C's.

My history teacher, Mr. Jones, at Johnson Jr. High School was another Buzz Lightyear-type and another black male who awakened my mind to possibilities. My "beyond" was launched by Mr. Jones and propelled me beyond the puzzle of mathematics and the disinterest in the all-consuming world of basketball that seemed to exist in the projects.

What was a black kid in the projects to do if he didn't like basketball? Actually, I despised round ball, as it seemed that was all we had for athletics in school. Everyone played NBA-style basketball all year round, on the playground and during school gym. Oh, we did climb ropes on occasion during gym class and participated in a few other nonsense exercises, but basketball was it. I was lanky and uncoordinated as well as a nerd. There wasn't anyone to coach me in the fine art of dribbling and crossover control. I was certain one had to be born, endowed or otherwise received a special blessing from the God of Hoops to have skills to take it down the lane.

This was not the environment for a Woody or a Buzz Lightyear. Consequently, I so disliked gym that joining cross-country track was the perfect strategy for bypassing B-ball. Hey, I had already perfected the art of long running from my early years of being chased. Running track became a learned extension of who I was. Our cross-country team was in last place or next to last at every meet until I ran in high school. Running in whatever T-shirt, shorts and tennis shoes we had, added to our last place finish, I was certain. It's the embarrassment factor in play. In a way, winning really didn't matter since I knew I was fast and had respectable endurance for the sport.

I DISCOVERED A NEW REALM OF THE "ME" THROUGH MR. JONES and American history in the 9th grade. I had this peculiar and innate ability to retain facts, dates, and history. I simply loved stuffing my brain and spilling it out in perfect recall. It didn't appear as though anyone had mastered memory which seemed to be happenstance or an annoyance at best on any given school day. I realized this aptitude created momentum as it became a personal challenge. This aptitude became a ticket out of the projects, one that I didn't credit until after the fact. It was the beginning of an end and the start of a new beginning.

During one class, Mr. Jones discussed the Civil War and the Gettysburg Address. I was surprised how strongly those hallowed words struck my social consciousness, given the world that occupied me. Like Buzz, I became single-minded and eagerly took it as a personal challenge to memorize Lincoln's stirring speech given on the grounds of a cemetery in Gettysburg, Pennsylvania. I recited his speech the very next day in class and still remember much of it today. Unfortunately, I failed to consider the consequences of my self-discovery. A few well-placed punches and general harassment after school helped to remind me of the penalties of learning more than some students appreciated or supported. No matter—something had been released that would follow me through secondary schooling, into college, summer jobs, and well into my career.

Another learning and significant soul winning plus was realizing what caused my mother to smile in the otherwise bleak place where our family was derailed. Report card time was especially rewarding and became my personal way of "taking it to the hoop" but in a positive and productive means of earning my props. Mom would smile, I would feel better about myself, and so the cycle continued. I remembered everything. History befriended Science, then Social Studies, Art, and most every subject that wasn't Math.

Developing a dogged attitude during school presented an interesting lesson for my first job as a fifteen-year-old teenager. It didn't take a Buzz mentality or belief or an undying mission in life to work this first job. I wanted to work to earn my own money. My mother's job as a nursing assistant didn't pay enough to pass out money between five kids. We didn't receive an allowance but would get some left-over change on occasion.

I took it upon myself at age fifteen to apply for a summer job through the public housing facility located at the corner of Stanton Rd and Alabama Ave in southeast D.C. Honestly, it was an embarrassing job, being a street sweeper in a gang of broom pushers for approximately six weeks during one summer in D.C. A group of a dozen or so teenagers were assembled at a staging area and then directed to an even worst public housing site within walking distance of my project. For the most part we sat on the curb until someone in our disparate group sighted a supervisor driving up. We didn't spring into action to fool our supervisor. Sweepers and brooms seemed to more lazily fall into the stance signalling we were about to do work. The supervisor slowed to a crawl never stopping. He practiced "drive-by" leadership. A few words of acknowledgement that followed seemed to satisfy job requirements for our supervisor. Out of an unintentional respect, we looked busy until his vehicle was thirty or forty yards past the group, then we returned to our position of sitting and lingering on the curb. I knew better than to do any work unless others were pushing brooms.

I became accustomed to moderating my enthusiasm by now, so sweeping assumed a strategic look of being nonchalant and indifferent. I could push a broom while others sat about, just if it wasn't done with purpose and reward. I made it appear as though I was angry and frustrated at the dirt and debris. To anyone passing by, it had to look as if my true motivation was singularly focused on receiving bi-weekly checks. It was the worst first employment that anyone could have had, and I was convinced no future pay was worth the boredom and sheer lack of interest and motivation.

WE EVENTUALLY MOVED OUT OF THE PROJECTS BY THE TIME I started high school. Funny, the one thing I should remember most and celebrate, I have no recollection of. I just recall one day living on Shipley Terrace as if being born again. I don't recall a moving truck or family hauling furniture and belongings from one place to another. We were still in southeast D.C. and less than a mile from the projects. Nonetheless, it was if the family moved on up and out of state.

Finally, unabridged fun and freedom opened up like light through a darkened prism. My greatest saving grace was that none of my mortal adversaries, like the evil Emperor Zurg who tormented Buzz, ever made it to high school. I don't know where they made it to or if they waited for fresh nerds and the uninitiated. How can one ever be uninitiated if he lived in the projects? I was fully in love with high school even though it was necessary to travel through the gauntlet of mine fields of my former projects every morning and afternoon.

Living on Shipley Terrace served as a gateway to possibilities. Granted, I wasn't necessarily emboldened with my first job but figured it was worth another try. At age sixteen, I walked into the Washington Animal Hospital on Pennsylvania Avenue. I had never had a pet as our family lived in apartments nearly all of my life. There was one rabid-like German Shepard shackled to a tree out back of the two-story apartment my aunt lived in. The heavy chain links kept human and beast at safe distance from what was surely Stephen King's inspiration for writing *Cujo*, the 1981 horror novel about a rapid dog.

My lack of familiarity with animals didn't deter me. A heavily accented English couple owned the veterinary hospital. I think they warmed to me because like them, I didn't quite seem to fit in with my surroundings. Besides being a kennel hand, feeding animals and cleaning cages for up to fifty or more animals, I learned to develop x-rays, help doctors during examinations, and was even able to stand at a distance to observe surgical operations. I was always curious and intrigued by new things.

There was one oddity that I didn't expect to find, working in the back of the animal clinic. There was a dog groomer and he was a black man. I laughingly thought this was not a legal profession or at least an acceptable job for a black man. Maybe his family and friends had no idea of his real money-making scheme. He maintained a finely manicured goatee and small thinning afro. He always entered or exited from a back door. Our relationship consisted of my bringing him regular doggie customers or pets matted and tangled, meeting the groomer for the first time. I would then return them to the owners who were enthralled with the makeover. I didn't get to know him as he didn't seem interested in knowing me. I only knew him as the black guy in the back of the clinic.

I really appreciated the trust and encouragement given me by my immigrant employers. I learned responsibility and commitment which would serve me well in summer jobs to follow. I worked those kennels alone on Sundays for nearly two years and eventually grew tired of the routine. Truth be told, one day I was lending a hand in holding down a large and older German Sheppard in order to take an x-ray of his arthritic hip. The combination of being stretched in an awkward position; the apparent pain and fear caused him to bite through his muzzle. I just so happen to be on the biting end. My left wrist still bares the scare from that encounter. It was then that I decided something safer and more interesting was needed.

Rex: *What're we gonna do, Buzz?*
Buzz *Lightyear: Use your head!*
Rex: *But I don't wanna use my head!*

This exchange occurred as Buzz was figuring out how to break through an air vent in order to rescue his friends. Rex didn't want to use his head as a battering ram. I, on the other hand, had learned from my days in junior high school that my head — my brain—was my best tool.

Working at the animal hospital was my first real job and one that reinforced the idea that all I had to do was search out that which interested me and take a crack at it. Perhaps a little audaciousness and determination played into it. I do believe being naïve was an asset. I didn't succumb to any discouragements or beliefs that my attempts for personal growth was misguided and unrealistic. In many ways, there wasn't anything to lose since I didn't have that next job to begin with. How could I forfeit that which I didn't have?

I was aware that the Naval Research Laboratory (NRL) in the southwest corner of D.C. was hiring for summer positions. The NRL is aligned with the Office of Naval Research and became part of a consolidating effort that brought existing Navy Research, Development, Test, and Evaluation Engineering and Fleet Support facilities together in 1992. The facility provided a broad base of scientific and technologic research. It also provided support functions, developed new materials, techniques, equipment, and systems.

I was a junior in high school (1974 – 1976) by this point, and the idea of working at a research facility was appealing. I was a member of the base supply department. It didn't quite measure up to the job of research and development that I had in mind, but it was a start.

Our department supplied electrical, fittings, plumbing, tools, fixtures, and hundreds of other parts needed by the trades on base to maintain the facility. The lab was in many ways self-supported with its own work crews exclusively assigned to the base. All of this was necessary for scientists and specialists to conduct research and development. The supply building was large and open with rows upon rows of bins filled with every part imaginable. It had to be an electrician's or plumber's paradise.

My lofty job, along with several other summer interns, was to keep track of inventory. We received and counted new stock, replenished stock bins and had periodic days where all the inventory in our building was required to be accounted for or otherwise counted. Can you imagine counting the number of nuts or washers that were in an open bin that could hold several hundred at any given time? There were easily several hundred stock bins containing various size items. Again, not my finest research work but it paid well ahead of minimum wage for summer jobs. I was in the big time for summer income but in the doldrums for challenge.

I knew from my summer broom job, that idle hands and mind made for a very long day. My solution was simply silly and senseless but uniquely me. I started playing games to help pass the day and be productive in the inventory department. There I was—this seventeen-year-old lanky six-foot-tall teenager, sporting a thick afro and shining skin due to oily skin and productive acne, entertaining himself with childish play.

How fast could I count a hundred items? Guess how may pipe elbows were in a bin and see how close I came to the actual count. Could I complete inventory on a given bin within fifteen minutes? If I needed a restroom break, how much more could I inventory before nearly peeing down my leg?

I was getting through my inventory accurately and at such a pace that one day my supervisor told me to follow him to the department office. Sitting in a designated chair behind closed doors, he told me in a matter of fact tone that I was working too much and too fast. He made it plainly clear, just in case, that I was making everyone else look bad because most had been working in the supply department for years but had not worked through inventory as quickly as me.

I remember thinking, "How was I supposed to know?" My intention was to stay awake on my feet verses showing up others. As I sat there, I wondered if I was experiencing the street sweeping job in disguise. Nevertheless, I appreciated the chance to work somewhere other than McDonald's, the grocery store or if you were lucky, at Sears. That year, much to my surprise, the department head submitted my name for consideration for the CAPSO-N Certificate of Merit and Special Achievement Award along with a monetary award, which I and several other interns at the naval base received.

I WAS ALL BUT GUARANTEED A JOB AT THE NAVAL RESEARCH Center the next year. Therefore, I decided to apply to a different area and was selected as a member of the Solution Chemistry Section, Inorganic and Electrochemistry Branch of the Chemistry Division. Honestly, I had no idea what to expect or the type of work a summer intern would do. At least it sounded interesting and important. Oh, how it became way more than interesting.

I didn't have a chemistry class in high school and now I was in college—it wasn't required. Yet one of the scientists, Dr. Venesky made time to visit and talk about a career at the research facility. He saw something in me and cultivated my inquisitive nature and willingness to accept new challenges. He was quite a mentor and had a lasting effect on my life. During the two summers I worked there, I learned to conduct experiments used to develop a particular reclamation process. My work involved following a precise series of steps using different and sometimes caustic chemicals, spectrometers and other equipment. I recorded every aspect of my daily experiments and resulting test results. The white lab coat and my lab room, which was housed in a door less vault, gave me a sense of self-worth and a belief that I could contribute to a larger and meaningful effort.

I received a CAPSO-N and Special Achievement Award along with a monetary gift for the two summers at the laboratory. I still have the August 28, 1978 "Labstracts" (Vol. XVIII, No. 34) which was the internal newspaper for the base. The photo of me receiving awards from Dr. Fred E. Saalfeld, Superintendent of the Chemistry Division, showed this young, skinny teenager smiling with pride. I remembered how my mother seemed to emanate respect for me; her proud grin and how special those moments became to me. There wasn't much to be cheerful about, so her warmth and the invisible words written on her face are still secure in my bank of positive memories.

By now I was in college at Norfolk College, which later became Norfolk State University (NSU). I was at Norfolk College because it was the best option out of the three options offered to me by my mother. I could join the Army, work at McDonald's or go to college. I knew many who headed off to the armed services with the hopes of using the G.I. Bill to pay for a college degree. Others joined up because there wasn't anything more inter-esting available. Toward the end of high school, I grew tired of schooling and frankly lacked motivation to search for the next step in my life. College seemed like the better option, especially compared to work in a fast food restaurant. Mom wasn't going to allow me to sit at home without a job if I didn't go to college. Intuitively, I knew that as well.

I'm thankful that my brother was already attending NSU and was in his senior year. I hadn't bothered to study for the SAT test because there was still a secret and unspoken part of me that just didn't want to attend four or more years of additional schooling. Resolved to meet my mother's requirements, I applied to NSU maybe slightly upset to discover I was accepted. I hadn't figured out what to major in, so for two years, I majored in general courses. Which degree program would define who I would become? The search began.

By this time in my life, I had joined campus Christian groups, had a sense of being an improved member of society and possessed an insatiable urge to give something back in life. My first exploration was with social work. I interviewed with a grossly overworked social worker in Norfolk, Virginia. The building housed clouds of cigarette smoke produced by and enveloping overworked and miserable looking social workers. I was taken aback by the atmosphere of depression and hopelessness in that place. I could feel in the social worker I met with, the remnants of genuine intentions. Unfortunately, purpose was submerged under stacks of case files, low pay, and a certain futility which may have explained the glazed-over look. Or was that the look after years of exposure to direct and second-hand smoke?

I thought it was within me to become a social worker martyr, but I needed to be certain. At the suggestion of the social worker, I began mentoring an elementary school kid with Attention Deficit Hyperactivity Disorder (ADHD). Imagine my surprise as this bright, but over-the-top child completely wore down my noble intention. I was defeated by an eight-year-old whose attention span was about ten seconds. My mentoring time was exhausting and short. My career search continued.

I was nearing the end of my sophomore year, having taken almost every general course offered while deciding my life's ambition. One day I wondered into the Mass Communications Department. There I watched through a glass observation area as students deliver television productions for mid-term grades. One frantic student raced outside the studio begging for someone to stand in for his absent announcer. All they needed was someone to read a script into a microphone. I volunteered, and it just so happened that my baritone voice wasn't afraid of a microphone. I hung out, observing through the glass in between classes and whenever possible. Soon I was sought out to serve as announcer for other student productions.

My plunge into radio began. I had the most excitement, fun and personal achievement during the last two years of college before graduation. I was elected as the Student President of the Communications Association, became the first program manager for our brand-new educational radio station (later turned into a music format). I was a radio announcer, producer and executive producer. I loved radio production and produced a fifteen- minute radio program, which aired on a local radio station down the street from NSU. What a rush!

There were tangible and nurturing characters that joined forces in the success in my life. They entered and continued to liberate me from my past. They freely and energetically contributed toward my future. My professors and my time in the General Education Department at NSU contributed to my growing confidence and I learned behavior and actions:

> "Work hard, respect others, accept that others can and are willing to complement your life, and understand you can't approach life solely on your own intellect and devices."

The hosts of supporting players in my life were many. Mrs. Battle from the General Education Department became a friend and advocate for me. She saw to it that I received a part-time paying position in General Ed. She also guided me in securing financial aid. Consequently, three of my four years at NSU where covered by grants and scholarships. I had loans totalling slightly over $1500 after four years of college.

Maybe my experience with radio could be parleyed into my next adventure. "You never know until you ask" held a certain truth in the statement. My next job application was for a summer intern position through the Department of Interior and the Department Parks and Recreation. Inconceivable as it was, the summers of 1979 and 1980 found me working as a park technician/intern for the White House tour program in D.C. How cool was that? We wore olive green Park Ranger uniforms with the official embroider emblems. Spit shinned black shoes (at least I spit on mine) were topped only by the wide brim park ranger hat and police-like walkie-talkie. I was as cop-like as one could get without having a gun and handcuffs. Again, how cool was this? As a park technician, we had no authority to arrest, ticket or exercise any police actions. Nevertheless, the uniform created the impression that we did. The perception helped to move people along the tour route and stopped car traffic when necessary.

You should know that I salivated at the thought of holstering a police special to complete the intimidating look. Finally, I was the one who was in control or at least carried the look. It probably was a good thing interns weren't issued weapons.

As a park intern in our official uniforms, we were responsible for managing all aspects of tours leading up to the doors of the White House. This included ticket distribution, crowd control, escorting tour groups (7,000 plus tourists during peak periods within a four to five-hour time slot) and providing general information about tourist sites in the D.C. and surrounding areas.

There were two especially exhilarating and gratifying facets of my summer internship. My radio style voice and friendly ranger-like demeanor gave me the chance to share in introducing national and international performing groups while visitors waited under canopied bleachers in a staging area on the Ellipse just south of the White House. High school and college bands along with musical bands from the armed services and groups from other countries were featured. This was my nirvana. I was on stage, talking to hundreds of tourists at a time. I was the self- proclaimed smooth "Barry White" voice of the National Park Services.

Another rare experience for me, while working with the White House visitor program, was the opportunity to travel without leaving D.C. I would have preferred to visit England, India, Germany, Brazil, or Denmark, to name a few. However, my family never won the lotto and the modest income only allowed us welcomed relief from being classified as welfare recipients. Instead of traveling to foreign countries, residents of these interesting and distant places visited my city and talked to me in the bleachers or while in line waiting to enter the White House. I genuinely enjoyed talking with these eloquent visitors from England, speed talkers from India, and polite residents of Japan. Sometimes, cultures clashed, and some tourists were rude with unrealistic demands. I still found those two years to be worth the blistering sun and humidity in the heat of a July and August summers.

College graduation came too fast. Now what was I to do? I had married the month after graduating college as my wife and I were now expecting our first child. Working in radio was "my thing" but low pay was the price and privilege of working at a local station. It was great experience and the perfect resume-building work. However, the pay couldn't begin to support a soon to be growing family.

With my Bachelor of Science degree in Communications, my wife and I headed off to Ohio State University (OSU) with a full scholarship and stipend to work on a master's degree in Communications. I thought that maybe I could teach at a college level and retain that state of "nirvana" found at Norfolk State University.

Not more than a half semester into my first year at OSU, I accepted that a master's program was not meant to be my new direction. Therefore, with determination, I took my background from sweeping streets, cleaning kennels at the animal hospital, to gaining experiences from every job in order to become . . . wait for it . . . a life insurance divisional underwriting trainee for a major multiline mutual insurance company. There was not a crystal ball that could have come close to predicting this next step.

I've shared my educational background several times when speaking to groups about life underwriting or insurance during my career. After sharing my broadcasting experience and seeing heads nod, acknowledging my deep, resonating, announcer-type voice, I jokingly say that "I've made it!" In other words, working in insurance wasn't what my degree in broadcast communications was preparing me to do. Yet in a way, the degree and other life experiences combined to prepare me for varied or any pursuits.

My path coursed along the life and health underwriting profession and into leadership. I moved from a first line supervisor in life and then in health underwriting, to a superintendent with both functions under my responsibility. Periodically, the corporate Vice President of underwriting talked with me about personal progress, constructive development and career advice and offered valuable insights.

We never agreed to a formal mentoring arrangement, nonetheless, I accounted the VP as a personal mentor and absorbed everything I could from those meetings. The next career step was that of an Assistant Vice President of Life/Health Underwriting, as my mentor's replacement. I recall biographies of a few leaders who started in the mailroom of a company and ended up running the very same company as CEO. No, I didn't run the company. However, I did prove it was possible to start as a trainee and end up leading the very same department that launched a career. My success was directly attributed to previous jobs but also to the coaching and leadership of this wonderful leader and friend.

During the last several years of my career, I moved into leading the Life and Health Claims Department of the same insurance company. It's worth noting that I not only made it out of Washington, D.C. but my career also carried me and family to Ohio, Maryland, Virginia, Illinois, Colorado, and back to Illinois over nearly a thirty-seven-year career in life and health insurance.

I didn't envision underwriting and Claims as a next step, but it has and continues to be my greatest adventure. "To Infinity and beyond" was the energetic pronouncement from Buzz Lightyear. Some might say my life represents an "infinity and beyond" or rags to riches outcome. Perhaps in a certain light that is the case. But from my view, success was found by embracing the belief that determination, fortitude, personal discovery, and wise coaching created the environment for overcoming my project beginning—my "unnecessary roughness". Many mentors as well as others that I looked up to poured into my life and created opportunities. I'm forever grateful to the band of supporters and mentors.

I continue to search forward for my next adventures, not forgetting the irreplaceable value of my past and how I, too, can lend experience and lessons to support the next generations of broom sweepers to vice presidents.

16

BULLYING

"As adults, we all remember what it was like to see kids picked on in the hallways or in the schoolyard. And I have to say, with big ears and the name that I have, I wasn't immune. I didn't emerge unscathed".

— President Barack Obama

Admittedly, when researching the term bullying, it was difficult and initially unfair to relate what felt as my daily life and death struggle to hallway teasing and mocking behaviors. My cousin and confidant who witnessed my childhood life was quick to clarify that my experience was well beyond the common understanding of bullying. Surely, being punched, jumped and otherwise mauled by fellow students deserved a heightened or more critical grouping. Perhaps a special category for offenses including misdemeanors, felonies and attempted de-humanization would have been more appropriate. My punishments couldn't be attributed to some adults who accept "kids will be kids" which invariably minimizes the true potential for lifelong consequences. Nonetheless, I continued my education and understanding of the effects of bullying.

Initially, it appeared through online resources that a fairly consistent description of bullying is presented. The National Centre Against Bullying (www.ncab.org) defines bullying:

> *". . . bullying is when an individual or a group of people with more power, repeatedly and intentionally causes hurt or harm to another person or group of people who feel helpless to respond.*

- *More than one out of every five (20.8%) students report being bullied (National Center for Education Statistics, 2016).*

- *A meta-analysis of 80 studies analyzing bullying involvement rates (for both bullying others and being bullied) for 12-18 old students reported a mean prevalence rate of 35% for traditional bullying involvement and 15% cyberbullying (Modecki, Minchin, Harbaugh, Guerra, & Runions, 2014).*

- *Bullied students reported that bullying occurred in the following places: hallway or stairwell at school (42%), inside classrooms (34%), in the cafeteria (22%), outside of school grounds (19%), on the school bus (10%), and in the bathroom or locker room (9%). (National Center for Education Statistics, 2016).*

- *More than half of bullying situations (57%) stop when a peer intervenes on behalf of the student being bullied (Hawkins, Pepler, & Craig, 2001)*

- *The reasons for being bullied reported most often by students include physical appearance, race/ethnicity, gender, disability, religion, sexual orientation (National Center for Educational Statistics, 2016)."*

- Data from Pacer's National Bullying Prevention Center

It became clearer through further study that understanding bullying required a more expansive or broader view. It is disturbing to discover research conducted by the Secret Service and the U.S. Department of Education involving 37 school shootings including Columbine, find that about two-thirds of student shooters felt bullied, harassed, threatened or injured by others (American Psychological Association [APA], Oct. 29, 2004. www.apa.org). The APA article goes on to say that most bullying episodes don't result in school shootings, but it does underscore the serious nature of this social issue.

Preventingbullying.promoteprevent.org   alludes   to   the complexity of bullying. It says bullying must include three characteristics:

1. *Intentional – the behavior was aggressive and a deliberate attempt to hurt another person*
2. *Repeated – these aggressive actions occur repeatedly over time to the same person or group of people*
3. *Power imbalance – the person bullying has more physical or social power than the child or children bullied*

There is general agreement that bullying can involve kicking, pushing, hitting, damaging personal property, name calling (teasing, insults, racist and homophobic comments), and social dominance.

There are many online resources of which several will be shared at the end of this chapter. Some dictionaries also define a bully as an intimidator, behavior which is physically and mentally abusive, and even someone who is "blustering, quarrelsome, overbearing person who habitually badgers . . ."

I snickered mockingly at the idea of being badgered until realizing that it also means to be hassled and harassed. I was certainly harassed minimally on a daily basis or, so it seemed. Then followed by hitting on a less frequently but with regularity and punctuated with being jumped or beat up by a horde of guys on indiscriminate occasions. I guess there had to be some civility and graduated order even to abuses.

There is also social bullying. The Alannah & Madeline Foundation refers to social bullying as "covert" and can be more difficult to recognize. It says social bullying can include:

- *Lying and spreading rumors*
- *Negative facial or physical gestures*
- *Playing nasty jokes to embarrass and humiliate*
- *Mimicking unkindly*
- *Encouraging others to socially exclude someone*
- *Damaging someone's social reputation or social acceptance*

Today there is cyberbullying that makes use of social media (Facebook, Twitter, Snapchat, smartphones, etc.) to inflict hurtful messages.

The National Centre Against Bullying (www.ncab.org) provides a test of sorts to help your child determine if they are being bullied. The list of feelings strongly suggests the complexity and emotional consequences of bullying. The online site provides the following:

"If you're being bullied you might feel as if you:

- *Are scared to go to school, feel unsafe and afraid*
- *Can't sleep very well or have nightmares*
- *Don't want to be around family or friends*
- *Can't concentrate on your school or homework*
- *Seem to be getting into trouble all the time*
- *Are angry for no reason*
- *Are not very hungry or are extra hungry*
- *Suddenly have unexplained headaches or stomach-aches*
- *Are sad and down*
- *As though you're not worth much*
- *Are guilty*
- *Think what's happening is your fault (it isn't)*
- *Feel ashamed it's happening to you"*

I had many of those feelings but didn't know what to do or where to go for help. First Lady Michelle Obama said "It breaks our hearts to think that any child feels afraid every day in the classroom, on the playground, or even online" (Washington Post, March 11, 2011).

Some research (APA, Oct. 29, 2004) indicates those likely to be bullied might show certain characteristics including being quiet, withdrawn or shy, sensitive, insecure or suffer from low self-esteem. They may be physically weaker than the bully. "These characteristics are likely to be both a partial cause and a consequence of the bullying" according to the study.

Personally, I believe some kids are simply plant eaters like I was in junior high. Others are tormented even if they don't display these characteristics. Bullies don't discriminate as such but they do seem to look for easy targets. Regardless, it's evident for my personal situation that bullying might have at least been minimized by standing up for myself despite being afraid.

> *"One's dignity may be assaulted, vandalized and cruelly mocked, but it can never be taken away unless it is surrendered"*

Now what? Where do we go from recognizing potential signs of bullying?

Undoubtedly, parents, teachers and school administrators must work in concert and as curators of student's emotional well-being. The American Psychological Association (APA) featured an interview with Susan Swearer, PhD. The April 2, 2010 interview and article "Bullying: What Parents, Teachers Can Do to Stop It". Dr. Swearer also co-edited "Bullying in North American Schools" which was in print at the time of the interview. She is an expert in bullying and is an associate professor of School Psychology at the University of Nebraska-Lincoln in the Department of Educational Psychology.

Dr. Swearer offers solutions to address the growing concerns with bullying. Most significant is the awareness of signs of bullying and immediate intervention by parents and teachers. She also emphasizes the need to help children feel safe and to have a support network.

Several steps were created by the Alannah & Madeline Foundation's National Centre Against Bullying and can serve as a guide to parents, teachers and children. These steps are repeated here in its entirety:

1. *Recognize that bullying matters – because it hurts in the short and long term. It's everybody's responsibility.*
2. *Be clear about what bullying is. It is an ongoing misuse of*

power in relationships through repeated aggressive verbal, physical and/or social behavior online or offline, which intends to cause physical and/or psychological harm, distress or fear. Bullying almost always occurs alongside cyber bullying.

3. *Bullying is not mutual conflict between equals, single acts of nastiness or aggression or social rejection or dislike unless it is deliberate, repeated and intended to cause distress.*

4. *Watch for the following signs because many children will rarely say what is happening to them (trouble at school, drop in academic performance, sleep and/or eating disorders, withdrawal from social activities).*

5. *Never ignore a bullying or cyber bullying situation. Respond to it as a parent or teacher with respectful listening, noting down the particulars of the situation and how the young person wants it resolved. Usually they are not interested in punishing the person who is bullying them; they just want it to stop.*

6. *Encourage young people to tell someone who can help and not to ignore bullying; it will not go away on its own.*

7. *Explain to young people that retaliating physically or aggressively will usually make things worse.*

8. Strategies young people can practice to cope with bullying include walking away, acting unimpressed, or pretending not to notice. Online strategies can include blocking, strategic ignoring of the behavior and saving evidence via screenshots.

9. *Encourage young people to have diverse friendship groups. It's too easy to be excluded or sidelined if you only have a couple of friends.*

10. *If bullying or cyber bullying is particularly serious (physical or deeply personal), the Office of the Children's eSafety*

Commissioner or the police can be contacted. Before then, you might want to contact Kids Helpline on 1-800-551-800.

For more information, visit:

www.ncab.org.au/bullying-advice/

www.stopbullying.gov

www.infoaboutkids.org

www.pacerteensagainstbullying.org

17

NEVER THE END

UNNECESSARY ROUGHNESS. WHAT'S THE ROUGHNESS IN YOUR PAST or present? Maybe you were bullied, became pregnant at an early age, suffered from depression, or had suicidal thoughts. It could have been that you were a child who had to care for a brother or sister. Maybe a different direction was carved out of your life; like a light-weight raft uncontrollably thrown about by a raging river. Perhaps some dysfunctional family surroundings played out a scheme of neglect, drugs or other abuses. A stupid mistake or reckless judgment resulting in dropping out of school or years of incarceration are unfortunately common consequences in society today.

The magnitude of those choices may still be felt today and will certainly be never forgotten. Whatever is the cause for your abrasive life, if this skinny, shy, nerdy, and ill-prepared kid could rise above an unwanted destiny in the projects, then you too, can realize similar heights.

Carly Fiorina, the former Chief Executive Officer for Hewlett-Packard once said,

"People's ideas and fears can make them small but they cannot make you small. People's prejudices can diminish them but they cannot diminish you. Small-minded people can think they determine your worth. But only you can determine your worth."

It does take a certain courage to reach around, over, through or past your fears and self-loathing. Some might have given up on their higher expectations and replaced them with discontent. Yet pushing a street broom can lead to cleaning kennels in an animal hospital; the kennel can lead to a navy research facility, a White House summer job, and....I think you get the picture. There doesn't have to be an end to living beyond your unnecessary roughness.

ABOUT THE AUTHOR

Wendell P. Haywood (he goes by Wendell P.) lives in Bloomington, Illinois. He retired in 2017 from an executive position after nearly thirty-seven years in the insurance industry with a top 500 Company in the U.S.

He has five wonderful boys, three fantastic daughters-in-law and six highly energetic grandchildren. Wendell enjoys reading, biking, and working with children.

Wendell has been writing short stories and poems since he was in elementary school. This is his first published book. He can be reached at wphaywood0919@gmail.com.

Made in the USA
Lexington, KY
30 January 2019